# THE UK AIR FRYER COOKBOOK

*250 Affordable, Delicious, Easy & Healthy Recipes That the Whole Family Will Love!*

By

Fearne Prentice

## A BOOK FROM THE
# COOKING WITH FEARNE
### SERIES

# A BOOK FROM THE
# COOKING WITH FEARNE
## SERIES

**The Air Fryer will change the way we cook and eat forever!**

If you already got "The UK Air Fryer Cookbook for Beginners", then this book is the perfect next step to master Air Fryer cooking.

This book consists of 12 different sections, each complete with comprehensive recipes and a list of required ingredients. You'll never need another Air Fryer cookbook again!

Thank you for buying this book by Fearne Prentice today, and don't forget to stay tuned for more recipes under the "Cooking with Fearne" series!

# DON'T FORGET THAT THIS PURCHASE COMES WITH A FREE BOOK!

**How To Access Your BONUS Coloured Photos & Beautifully Designed Bonus Book For the Top Recipes:**

To keep printing costs down, we sadly couldn't include coloured pictures inside this print book, otherwise we would've had to charge at least triple the price if not more.

So, to make sure you still have access to coloured photos, we have created a PDF version of the top recipes from this book with supplementary images, completely free for you.

*Just follow the steps below to access it via the QR Code (found inside the book upon purchase), or click the link if you are reading this on your Phone / Device.*

1. *Unlock your phone & open up the phone's camera*

2. *Make sure you are using the "back" camera (as if you were taking a photo of someone) and point it towards the QR code at the bottom of the page.*

3. *Tap your phone's screen exactly where the QR code is.*

4. *A link / pop up will appear. Simply tap that (and make sure you have internet connection) and the FREE PDF containing the coloured images should appear.*

5. *You now have access to this whenever you want, simply bookmark it or download it and you can take it wherever you want!*

**We hope this makes up for not being able to print with coloured photos and that you love the recipes! Thank you!**

# TABLE OF CONTENTS

# 1 | INTRODUCTION

## AUTHOR'S NOTE

Fussy meals are for the old days. Thankfully, with appliances like the air fryer, the possibilities of cooking sumptuous foods in little time and less effort are endless. That's what I aim for in this cookbook.

I won't be excessive with how unique the air fryer is or how much better than a deep fryer it is. Many blogs confirm so many positive words about it already. Rather, this cookbook focuses on bringing all that talk to life through remarkable dishes.

Maybe you were gifted an air fryer over the holidays, or maybe you recently purchased one but still struggle to churn out delicious meals with it. This cookbook is for you.

There's no need to just use it for baking potatoes or keeping a close embrace to the crispy bacon you repeatedly bake. Not that they are bad. But in this cookbook, I share over 250 of my favourite delicious, healthy, and affordable meals that you can make with your air fryer – no matter the size that you have.

My desire is to simplify your life by offering an overload of recipes so that your air fryer pumps out something tasty all year round.

That said, you're probably curious to know what's in store for you, so I'll let you have your way.

Head on! Enjoy each process, flavour, taste, and repeat.

## A LITTLE WALK THROUGH THE COOKBOOK

Things are pretty straightforward in this cookbook – sometimes with a little elaboration – so you can get the steps right. My mission is that whatever recipe you make from this cookbook turns out scrumptious, no matter your cooking level.

So there are recipes for beginner air fryer users or cooks, the moderate one, and the expert who may choose to tweak things for their version. I love ease and creativity all in one.

This cookbook packs 250+ recipes that are a spin between affordable, delicious, easy, and healthy foods that are perfect for everyone. You will find recipes that are unique to kids, options for plant-based dietary needs, and offer you a plethora of food options that fit daily and even festive needs. There's really no excuse as to why your kitchen should be empty of mouth-watering foods.

## WHY DID I CHOOSE THE AIR FRYER?

Clearly because it is convenient and can replace many other appliances all in one. In a period where managing resources is crucial, zoning towards the air fryer makes life all the better – not to mention the counter space it saves you.

You can bake with it, roast something smoky and savoury, grill, dehydrate, create stir-fries, and its forte, fry crispier foods than a deep fryer – all the while using the least amount of oil possible. (Note: you will need a stovetop for prepping meals in some of the recipes shared here.)

The air fryer is the perfect family appliance, saving you  time so you can focus on other important things. With the air fryer, you also have better control of cooking. You'll find that food rarely burns with it as you can conveniently manage the temperature and time settings, and check how food is cooking as you go.

By now, you hopefully sense that creating all 250+ recipes with my air fryer was a breeze. I can't wait to share them with you!

## A LITTLE GUIDE FOR USING YOUR AIR FRYER AND THE COOKBOOK

I would always suggest you read the manual that your air fryer came with, as it is a much better guide that I could possibly pack in this cookbook. Some basics, however, apply to all.

Preheating is key when using your air fryer. Like baking in the oven, creating a heat conducted space helps your food cook under the right temperature and doneness. However, not to bore you through the recipe, I skipped mentioning "preheat the air fryer" and went straight for the chase, i.e., the exact cooking temperature and time. **Always preheat the air fryer for 3 to 5 minutes or as your manual instructs** before introducing your food to it and using the temperature and time that the recipe requires.

The recipes in this cookbook are a merge between baked, grilled, roasted, dehydrated, and fried foods, and in some cases, require using certain accessories, like baking dishes, foil, cake pans, muffin trays, etc. These accessories are all safe for the air fryer. Just ensure that you find the right material (silicone or aluminium will do) and check for the right size that fits the recipe.

The serving size here is set for four with a little run over in some recipes, making them the perfect amount for a small family. A standard air fryer should accommodate four servings in one cooking batch. For smaller air fryers, you may need to split your meal and bake them in batches.

Measurements offer metric and imperial styles with US cup comparisons too, so it's comfy for all. Here, I share a basic conversion table that you can refer to for accuracy. Otherwise, every recipe offers measurement comparisons so cooking is seamless.

# METRIC - IMPERIAL - US CONVERSION TABLE

**Volume conversions for liquids**

| METRIC | US CUPS | IMPERIAL |
|---|---|---|
| 15 ml | 1 tablespoon | 1/2 fl oz |
| 30 ml | 1/8 cup | 1 fl oz |
| 60 ml | 1/4 cup | 2 fl oz |
| 80 ml | 1/3 cup | 2 1/2 fl oz |
| 120 ml | 1/2 cup | 4 fl oz |
| 160 ml | 2/3 cup | 5 fl oz |
| 180 ml | 3/4 cup | 6 fl oz |
| 240 ml | 1 cup | 8 fl oz |

**Weight conversions for dry ingredients**

| METRIC | US CUPS | IMPERIAL |
|---|---|---|
| 1/4 oz | 5/16 cup | 7 g |
| 1/2 oz | 1/16 cup | 15 g |
| 1 oz | 1/8 cup | 30 g |
| 2 oz | 1/4 cup | 60 g |
| 3 oz | 3/8 cup | 85 g |
| 4 oz | 1/2 cup | 110 g |
| 5 oz | 5/8 cup | 140 g |
| 6 oz | 3/4 cup | 170 g |
| 7 oz | 7/8 cup | 200 g |
| 8 oz | 1 cup | 225 g |
| 9 oz | 1 and 1/8 cups | 255 g |
| 10 oz | 1 and 1/4 cups | 280 g |
| 11 oz | 1 and 3/8 cups | 310 g |
| 12 oz | 1 and 1/2 cups | 340 g |
| 13 oz | 1 and 5/8 cups | 370 g |
| 14 oz | 1 and 3/4 cups | 400 g |
| 15 oz | 1 and 7/8 cups | 425 g |
| 1 lb | 2 cups | 450 g |

**Oven temperatures**

| Description | Electric degree C | Electric degree C Fan | Electric degree Farenheit | Gas Mark |
|---|---|---|---|---|
| Very cool | 110 | 90 | 225 | 1/4 |
| Very cool | 120 | 100 | 250 | 1/2 |
| Cool | 140 | 120 | 275 | 1 |
| Cool | 150 | 130 | 300 | 2 |
| Warm | 160 | 140 | 325 | 3 |
| Moderate | 180 | 160 | 350 | 4 |
| Moderately hot | 190 | 170 | 375 | 5 |
| Fairly hot | 200 | 180 | 400 | 6 |
| Hot | 220 | 200 | 425 | 7 |
| Very hot | 230 | 210 | 450 | 8 |
| Very hot | 240 | 220 | 475 | 9 |

## DOES THE AIR FRYER LIVE UP TO ITS NAME?

Not attempting to be a bearer of repetitive news, my first stance on the functionality of the air fryer is a great one.

Having gone through varying developments over the years, newer models of the air fryer prove to outperform many other appliances combined. I particularly love the air fryer for its counter saving space and sleek feel. It is an essential resource that is fantastic for all types of households. It lifts the burden of time wasting when cooking, reduces unhealthy eating options, and is multifunctional, hence making it high starred on my list of favourite appliances. I highly recommend it.

I believe the air fryer is here to stay, so it's about time we got to creating many fun recipes that we can make with it.

I hope these recipes will be a delight to explore.

As always, from my kitchen to yours, I wish you a swell time enjoying your air fryer and these recipes.

## FOODS YOU CAN COOK IN THE AIR FRYER

The air fryer will accommodate many solid foods like chicken, vegetables, nuts, red meats, seafood, etc. Thick liquids are better suited in casseroles, like creams and sauces. Runny liquids, like soups, would not be ideal as they may drip into the operating unit and cause damage.

The air fryer operates using technology that blows hot air over foods, helping air fry them for the extra crispy touch that you get. As such, it is better suited for foods that do not pack much liquid for quicker drying.

Always have some cooking spray on hand also. Most of the recipes require it for greasing to prevent food from sticking to the basket. Cooking spray also helps to keep your air fryer in good shape longer.

With these things said, how about we get into some recipes already?

# 2 | KID-TREATING BITES

*Managing kids – whether as
a parent, baby sitter, or aunty
– is indeed a labour of love.
Since the air fryer is great for
making the quickest bites,
these recipes are uniquely
created to be treats that chil-
dren will love.*

DON'T FORGET TO
GET THE

**TOP RECIPES** FROM
THIS BOOK AS

**A DOWNLOADABLE
PDF IN COLOUR**

# FOR FREE!

*KEEP READING TO FIND OUT
HOW!*

# CHEESY CORN FRITTERS

*Servings: 4*

**TOTAL CALORIES: 587**
Protein: 31.32g | Fats: 23.54g |
Carbs: 23.54g

## INGREDIENTS

- 225g (1 cup) gluten-free flour
- 60g (¼ cup) plain breadcrumbs
- 3g (½ tsp) garlic powder
- 3g (½ tsp) salt
- 1g (¼ tsp) ground black pepper
- 110g (½ cup) shredded cheddar cheese
- 340g (1½ cups) canned corn kernels, drained. Frozen but thawed is also fine.
- 2 eggs
- 45ml (3 tbsp) soured cream plus more for serving

## INSTRUCTIONS

1. In a bowl, mix the flour, breadcrumbs, garlic powder, salt, and black pepper. Add the corn kernels and cheddar cheese and mix evenly.
2. Crack the eggs into a bowl and whisk with the soured cream. Pour the mixture into the flour mixture and combine until the dough is sticky without any dry parts.
3. Line a baking sheet with parchment paper and set aside.
4. Using a cookie scoop, fetch some of the dough into your hands, roll into a ball, and then press into a mini fritter. Place the fritter on the baking sheet and make more mini fritters until the dough is finished.
5. Set the air fryer to 185°C (370°F) for 14 minutes.
6. Lay four corn fritters in the air fryer basket and lightly mist with cooking spray. Bake for 7 minutes per side or until golden brown.
7. Transfer the corn fritters to a wire rack and bake the remaining fritters.
8. Serve the corn fritters with more soured cream.

# CHICKPEA CHOCOLATE BLONDIES

*Servings: 4*

**TOTAL CALORIES: 391**
Protein: 13.51g | Fats: 15.75g |
Carbs: 51.91g

## INGREDIENTS

- 1 (400g / 15 oz) can chickpeas in water
- 1 egg, cracked into a bowl
- 60g (¼ cup) cashew butter or seed butter of choice
- 5g (1 tsp) vanilla extract
- 60g (¼ cup) gluten-free oats, dry
- 3g (½ tsp) baking powder
- 1g (¼ tsp) baking soda
- 30g (2 tbsp) granulated sugar
- 15g (1 tbsp) cinnamon powder
- 30g (2 tbsp) chocolate chips

## INSTRUCTIONS

1. Grease a square baking sheet (that can fit into your air fryer) with cooking spray. Put it aside.
2. In a food processor, add the chickpeas, egg, cashew butter, vanilla, oats, baking powder, baking soda, sugar, and cinnamon powder. Process until they form into a smooth thick dough.
3. Spread the dough onto the baking sheet and sprinkle on the chocolate chips. You can pat the chocolate chips into the dough to hold better if you prefer. Place the pan in the air fryer.
4. Set the air fryer to 175°C (350°F) for 10 minutes and bake for 10 minutes or until a toothpick inserted into the blondie comes out clean.
5. Take out the pan and let the blondie cool in it for 10 minutes. After, transfer the blondie onto a wire rack to cool completely.
6. Cut into squares and serve.

*THE UK AIR FRYER COOKBOOK*

## COCONUT-CRUSTED CHEESE BALLS

## EGG WHITE BITES

*Servings: 4*

**TOTAL CALORIES: 540**
Protein: 19.01g | Fats: 35.29g | Carbs: 38.81g

*Servings: 4*

**TOTAL CALORIES: 103**
Protein: 9.86g | Fats: 6.3g | Carbs: 1.25g

### iNGREDiENTS

- 55g (¼ cup) all-purpose flour / gluten-free flour
- 2 large eggs
- 225g (1 cup) shredded coconut
- 5g (1 tsp) chopped fresh parsley
- Salt to taste
- 12 mini mozzarella balls
- Cooking spray

### iNSTRUCTiONS

1. Pour the flour into a bowl, beat the eggs in another bowl, and mix the coconut, parsley, and salt on a plate.
2. Pat dry the mozzarella balls with a paper towel and dredge them in the flour. After, dip them in the eggs and coat them generously in the coconut-parsley mixture.
3. Set the air fryer to 175°C (350°F) for 10 minutes.
4. Lightly mist the air fryer basket with cooking spray and arrange the cheese balls in the basket in a single layer.
5. Fry the cheese balls for 8 to 10 minutes or until golden brown and crispy.
6. Plate the cheese balls and serve with tomato sauce.

### iNGREDiENTS

- 7 eggs, egg whites only
- 15ml (1 tbsp) double cream
- 15ml (1 tbsp) milk, type of choice
- 1g (¼ tsp) mustard powder
- Salt and black pepper to taste
- 55g (¼ cup) shredded cheddar cheese
- 2 green onions, sliced
- Cooking spray

### iNSTRUCTiONS

1. Crack the eggs and drain the egg whites into a bowl. Then whisk with the double cream, milk, mustard powder, salt, and black pepper until smooth. Add the cheddar cheese and green onions and mix until well spread around.
2. Mist an 8-holed silicone baking mould and fill with the egg mixture.
3. Set the air fryer to 170°C (340°F) for 12 minutes.
4. Place the mould in the fryer basket and bake for 10 to 12 minutes or until the egg whites set.
5. Take out the silicone mould and pop the egg white bites onto a serving plate.
6. Serve warm.

## GARLIC BUTTER POTATO BITES

(IN MINUTES)
PREP 10
COOK 18

*Servings: 4*

### TOTAL CALORIES: 179
Protein: 3.17g | Fats: 9.85g | Carbs: 22.09g

### INGREDIENTS

- 450g (1 lb) yellow potatoes, peeled
- 45g (3 tbsp) melted butter
- 15g (3 tsp) minced garlic
- 5g (1 tsp) dried basil
- Salt and black pepper to taste
- 5g (1 tsp) chopped fresh basil for garnish

### INSTRUCTIONS

1. In a bowl, combine the potatoes, butter, garlic, basil, salt, and black pepper. Toss well.
2. Set the air fryer to 200°C (400°F) for 18 minutes.
3. Spoon the potatoes into the air fryer basket, close the air fryer and cook for 18 minutes or until they are golden brown and tender, turning the potatoes after 9 minutes of cooking.
4. Pour the crispy potatoes into a serving bowl. Garnish with some basil and serve warm.

## GOLDEN RICE CRISP BITES

(IN MINUTES)
PREP 10
COOK 4

*Servings: 4*

### TOTAL CALORIES: 670
Protein: 3.38g | Fats: 116.45g | Carbs: 3.29g

### INGREDIENTS

- 110g (½ cup) salted butter plus some more for greasing
- 2 (200g / 10 oz) bags mini marshmallows
- 5g (1 tsp) vanilla extract
- 2kg (9 cups) toasted rice cereal

### INSTRUCTIONS

1. Grease a square baking sheet (that can fit into your air fryer) with butter. Put it aside.
2. Add the butter and marshmallows to a bowl and melt them in the microwave for 30 to 60 seconds. Stir them at 15 seconds intervals until the mixture is smooth.
3. Take out the bowl and pour the mixture into a bigger bowl. Stir in the vanilla first and then the rice cereal. Spread the mixture into the baking sheet, making sure to level well.
4. Set the air fryer to 170°C (340°F) for 3 minutes.
5. Place the baking sheet in the air fryer and toast for 1 to 3 minutes or until the rice crisps are golden brown.
6. Remove the baking sheet from the oven, let cool completely, and then refrigerate for 20 minutes.
7. Cut the rice crisps into squares and serve.

# HAM AND CHEESE POCKETS

*Servings: 4*

## TOTAL CALORIES: 709
Protein: 42.93g | Fats: 44.35g | Carbs: 32.76g

### INGREDIENTS

- 1 (8 oz) refrigerated crescent roll
- 24 ham slices
- 6 slices cheddar cheese
- 60g (¼ cup) melted butter for brushing

### INSTRUCTIONS

1. On a clean working surface, create 4 rectangles with the crescent dough – that is, pinching two triangles together and lightly stretching them.
2. Alternating ham and cheese, divide them onto one side of the rectangles – that would be 6 ham slices and 1½ cheese slices per rectangle.
3. Fold the empty side of the rectangles over the filling and seal the perforations. Also, brush both sides with butter.
4. Set the air fryer to 150°C (300°F) for 14 minutes.
5. Lay two pockets in the air fryer basket and bake for 12 to 14 minutes or until golden brown.
6. Transfer the ham and cheese pockets to a plate and bake the remaining ones.
7. Serve them warm as they are or pair them with mustard sauce.

# HONEYED WINGS

*Servings: 4*

## TOTAL CALORIES: 304
Protein: 14.69g | Fats: 14.32g | Carbs: 30.43g

### INGREDIENTS

- 8 chicken wings, separated at the joint
- 3g (½ tsp) salt or to taste
- 75g (1/3 cup) potato starch
- Cooking spray
- 60g (¼ cup) butter, melted
- 60g (¼ cup) honey
- 30g (2 tbsp) minced garlic

### INSTRUCTIONS

1. Set the air fryer to 160°C (380°F) for 25 minutes.
2. Season the chicken with salt and add them to a bowl. Pour on the potato starch and toss the chicken until they are well coated.
3. Mist the air fryer basket with cooking spray, lay in the chicken in a single layer, and lightly mist again with cooking spray.
4. Close the air fryer and fry for 25 minutes while shaking the basket once or twice during cooking. When the timer is done, set the temperature to 200°C (400°F) for 10 minutes. Cook the chicken for 5 to 10 more minutes or until golden brown and cooked within.
5. Remove the chicken into a bowl and set aside.
6. In another bowl, mix the butter, honey, garlic, and a pinch of salt. Mix well and pour over the chicken. Toss until the chicken is properly coated with the glaze.
7. Serve the chicken warm.

## LEMON CHICKEN BITES

(IN MINUTES)
PREP 15
COOK 12

*Servings: 4*

**TOTAL CALORIES: 292**
Protein: 19.36g | Fats: 22.27g | Carbs: 3.15g

### INGREDIENTS

- 450g (1 lb) chicken thighs, boneless and skinless
- 1g (¼ tsp) onion powder
- 3g (½ tsp) garlic powder
- 15g (1 tbsp) paprika
- 3g (½ tsp) chopped fresh parsley
- 5g (1 tsp) chopped fresh thyme
- 1g (¼ tsp) black pepper
- Salt to taste
- 15ml (1 tbsp) olive oil
- 30ml (2 tbsp) fresh lemon juice, divided
- Chopped fresh parsley for garnish

### INSTRUCTIONS

1. Using paper towels, pat dry the chicken and then cut into 2cm pieces.
2. Put them in a bowl and add the onion powder, garlic powder, paprika, parsley, thyme, black pepper, salt, olive oil, and half of the lemon juice. Mix the ingredients well until the chicken is properly coated with the seasoning.
3. Set the air fryer to 190°C (380°F) for 12 minutes.
4. Spoon the chicken pieces into the air fryer and cook for 8 to 12 minutes or until the chicken is golden brown. Meanwhile, shake the basket once or twice during cooking.
5. Transfer the chicken to a serving bowl and drizzle the remaining lemon juice on top. Garnish with some parsley and serve.

## MINI BATTERED SAUSAGES

(IN MINUTES)
PREP 10
COOK 12

*Servings: 4*

**TOTAL CALORIES: 937**
Protein: 37.57g | Fats: 72.47g | Carbs: 30.17g

### INGREDIENTS

- 100g + 50g (1 cup + ½ cup) all-purpose flour / gluten-free flour, divided
- 3g (½ tsp) baking soda
- 3g (½ tsp) salt or to taste
- 3g (½ tsp) black pepper or to taste
- 1 egg
- 250ml (1 cup) cold water
- 8 mini sausages, mildly flavoured
- Cooking spray

### INSTRUCTIONS

1. In a bowl, mix 100g (1 cup) of flour, baking soda, salt, and black pepper. Crack in the eggs, add the cold water, and whisk until smooth.
2. Dip the sausages into the batter, let the dripping batter fall off, and place them on a plate. Sprinkle them with the remaining flour on both sides and gently pat to adhere.
3. Set the air fryer to 180°C (390°F) for 10 minutes.
4. Lightly mist the air fryer basket with cooking spray and arrange the battered sausages in it. Lightly mist again with cooking spray.
5. Fry for 8 to 10 minutes, turning after 4 minutes of cooking on one side.
6. When they are golden brown, transfer them to a plate to slightly cool.
7. Serve them with some ketchup.

# MINI BEIGEL "BAGEL" PIZZAS

*Servings: 4*

## TOTAL CALORIES: 328
Protein: 16.12g | Fats: 7.65g | Carbs: 48.65g

### INGREDIENTS

- 4 mini bagel thins, plain flavour
- 30ml (2 tbsp) tomato sauce
- 110g (½ cup) shredded mozzarella cheese

### INSTRUCTIONS

1. Split the bagels by slicing them in halves. Now, lay them on a plate or tray with their inner sides facing upwards.
2. Thinly spread the tomato sauce on each and top with the mozzarella cheese (as much cheese as your child likes).
3. Set the air fryer to 200°C (400°F) for 6 minutes.
4. Lay the loaded bagels in the air fryer basket in a single layer (you can do this in batches) and cook for 4 to 6 minutes or until the cheese melts.
5. Plate the mini pizzas, then let them cool for about 4 minutes and serve.

# OATMEAL BITES

*Servings: 4*

## TOTAL CALORIES: 561
Protein: 21.84g | Fats: 10.27g | Carbs: 98.57g

### INGREDIENTS
- Cooking spray

To make the oatmeal cups:
- 1 ripe banana
- 450g (2 cups) oatmeal
- 60ml (¼ cup) applesauce
- 5ml (1 tsp) vanilla extract
- 30ml (2 tbsp) honey
- 3g (½ tsp) ground nutmeg
- 3g (½ tsp) ground cinnamon
- 1g (¼ tsp) ground ginger

For the filling and topping:
- 240ml (1 cup) yoghurt, flavour of choice
- A handful of fresh berries

### INSTRUCTIONS
To make the oatmeal cups:
1. Set the air fryer to 170°C (330°F) for 6 minutes. Then mist a 4-holed silicone muffin tray with cooking spray and set aside.
2. Peel the banana, add to a bowl, and mash with a fork until smooth. Afterward, stir in the oatmeal until smooth.
3. In a small bowl, mix the applesauce, vanilla, honey, nutmeg, cinnamon, and ginger until smooth. Pour the mixture on the oats and mix well.
4. Divide the oatmeal mixture into the muffin tray holes and use a spoon to line and shape the mixture into cups.
5. Place the tray in the air fryer and bake the oatmeal cups for 6 minutes or until they are golden brown.
6. Take out the tray and let oatmeal cups cool for 10 minutes in the holes. Afterward, remove them onto a wire rack.

For the filling and topping:
7. Fill the oatmeal cups with yoghurt to your desired quantity and add some berries.

# PANCAKE CHOCO-LATE BITES

*Servings: 4*

## TOTAL CALORIES: 564
Protein: 14.75g | Fats: 5.69g | Carbs: 111.59g

### INGREDIENTS

- 450g (2 cups) of your favourite pancake mix
- 360g (1½ cups) water, or half part each water and milk
- 120ml (½ cup) chocolate syrup

### INSTRUCTIONS

1. In a bowl, whisk the pancake mix and water, or water and milk, until smooth.
2. Fill an 8-holed silicone baking mould with the mixture.
3. Set the air fryer to 200°C (400°F) for 10 minutes.
4. Place the silicone mould in the air fryer and bake for 8 to 10 minutes or until the pancake bites set at the centre. You can check this by inserting a toothpick into them. If the toothpick comes out clean, then they are ready.
5. Take out the mould and let the pancakes cool in them for 10 minutes.
6. Meanwhile, fill a small piping bag with the chocolate syrup.
7. Pop the pancakes from the silicone mould and use a skewer to drill a hole into each pancake bite. Create a wide hole enough to take in as much chocolate as you'd like.
8. Cut a small slit at the mouth of the piping bag and press the chocolate syrup into each pancake piece.

# POPCORN CHICKEN

*Servings: 4*
*Marinating Time: 30 mins*

## TOTAL CALORIES: 782
Protein: 63.89g | Fats: 18.18g | Carbs: 86.53g

### INGREDIENTS
For the chicken and marinade:
- 900g (2 lb) chicken breast tenders
- 480ml (2 cups) almond milk
- 3g (½ tsp) paprika
- 5g (1 tsp) salt
- 3g (½ tsp) black pepper

For the dry ingredients:
- 680g (3 cups) all-purpose flour
- 10g (2 tsp) ground paprika
- 5g (1 tsp) kosher salt or to taste
- 10g (2 tsp) ground black pepper
- Cooking spray

For the mayo ketchup sauce:
- 120ml (½ cup) mayonnaise
- 15 to 30ml (1 to 2 tbsp) ketchup

### INSTRUCTIONS
For the chicken and marinade:
1. Cut the chicken into 2cm pieces and place them in a bowl. Pour on the almond milk and add the paprika, salt, and black pepper. Stir to coat the chicken very well. Cover the bowl with a napkin and refrigerate for 30 minutes.

For the dry ingredients:
2. On a plate, mix the flour, paprika, salt, and black pepper until smooth.

Making the popcorn chicken:
3. Take out the chicken from the refrigerator and uncover. Then, one after the other, remove each chicken from the marinade and dredge in the flour mixture. Lightly dip the chicken in the marinade again and generously coat with the flour mixture.
4. Set the air fryer to 190°C (380°F) for 12 minutes.
5. Mist the air fryer basket with cooking spray and arrange the chicken pieces in the basket in a single layer. You can do this in batches if your air fryer is small. Mist the chicken with some cooking spray and place the basket in the air fryer.
6. Cook for 10 to 12 minutes or until the chicken is golden brown and cooked within.
7. Remove the chicken onto a serving plate for serving.

Serve with mayo ketchup sauce:
8. In a bowl, mix the mayo and ketchup until smooth and pale pink.

# PRETZEL BITES

*Servings: 4*

## TOTAL CALORIES:613
Protein: 13.82g | Fats: 16.8g
| Carbs: 99.8g

### INGREDIENTS

- 480ml (2 cups) warm water, 43°C (110°F)
- 13g (2½ tsp) quick rise yeast
- 900g (4 cups) all-purpose flour / gluten-free flour + extra for dusting
- 5g (1 tsp) sea salt
- 15g (1 tbsp) granulated sugar
- Cooking oil
- 60g (4 tbsp) melted butter
- Flaky salt for garnish

### INSTRUCTIONS

1. In a bowl, mix the water and yeast until smooth.
2. In another bowl, mix the flour, salt, and sugar. Pour on the yeast liquid and combine until smooth thick dough forms.
3. Dust a working surface with flour, divide the dough into 8 pieces, and place on the surface. Roll each dough piece into a rope and cut into 2cm pieces.
4. Set the air fryer to 200°C (400°F) for 7 minutes.
5. Lightly mist the air fryer basket with cooking spray and lay the dough pieces in a single layer. You can do this in batches.
6. Close the air fryer and bake for 7 minutes or until the pretzel bites are light golden.
7. Remove the pretzel bites to a plate to cool and brush them with butter.
8. Sprinkle on some flaky salt and serve.

# SESAME-CRUSTED SALMON BITES

*Servings: 4*

## TOTAL CALORIES:260
Protein: 25.89g | Fats: 16.75g |
Carbs: 1.88g

### INGREDIENTS

- 450g (1 lb) salmon
- Salt and black pepper to taste
- 15ml (1 tbsp) olive oil
- 15ml (1 tbsp) fresh lemon juice
- 55g (¼ cup) sesame seeds
- Cooking spray

### INSTRUCTIONS

1. Using paper towels, pat dry the salmon, and then cut into 4cm pieces.
2. In a bowl, toss the salmon with salt, black pepper, olive oil, and lemon juice.
3. Spread the sesame seeds on a plate and one by one, coat the salmon pieces on each side with sesame seeds. Make sure to cover all sides of the salmon as much as possible.
4. Set the air fryer to 200°C (400°F) for 5 minutes.
5. Lightly mist the air fryer basket with some cooking spray and arrange the salmon pieces in the basket. Close the air fryer and fry for 4 to 5 minutes or until the golden brown and the salmon flaky within.
6. Remove the salmon onto a serving platter and serve.

# SWEET POTATO TOTS

*Servings: 4*

**TOTAL CALORIES:240**
Protein: 9.37g | Fats: 5.65g | Carbs: 38.01g

## INGREDIENTS

For this recipe, you will need to precook and mash some peeled sweet potatoes. Or if you'd prefer canned or bagged sweet potatoes, that's totally fine. Make sure the canned or bagged sweet potatoes are without unhealthy additives, however.

- 280g (1¼ cups) mashed sweet potatoes
- 60g (¼ cup) grated Parmigiano Reggiano cheese
- 170g (¾ cup) breadcrumbs, finely ground
- 4g (1½ tsp) garlic powder
- 10g (2 tsp) minced fresh chives
- 1g (¼ tsp) salt or to taste
- Cooking spray

## INSTRUCTIONS

1. In a bowl, combine the mashed sweet potatoes, Parmigiano Reggiano cheese, breadcrumbs, garlic powder, chives, and salt. Mix the ingredients until they are well combined.
2. Set a tray aside and start moulding the tots.
3. Scoop 15g (1 tbsp) of the sweet potato mixture into your hands and shape into a tot. Place it on the tray. Continue making tots using the remaining mixture.
4. Set the air fryer to 190°C (370°F) for 8 minutes.
5. Mist the air fryer basket with cooking spray and arrange the tots in it without overlapping. Lightly mist the tots again. You can cook them in batches.
6. Close the air fryer and fry each batch for 6 to 8 minutes or until the tots are golden brown and hold their shape.
7. Transfer the tots to a serving plate and serve them with some ketchup.

# TOFU POPPERS

*Servings: 4*

**TOTAL CALORIES:672**
Protein: 23.41g | Fats: 14.83g | Carbs: 110.5g

## INGREDIENTS

For the tofu poppers:
- 1 (200g / 7 oz) extra-firm tofu, pressed
- 110g (½ cup) all-purpose flour / gluten-free flour
- 120ml (½ cup) water (or a little more if too thick)
- 30ml (2 tbsp) maple syrup
- 450g (2 cups) breadcrumbs
- Cooking spray

Pair with coriander cream:
- 120ml (½ cup) soured cream
- 15ml (1 tbsp) chopped fresh coriander

## INSTRUCTIONS

To make the tofu poppers:
1. Cut the tofu into 2 to 4cm cubes.
2. In a bowl, mix the whole wheat flour, water, and maple syrup until smooth and it coats the back of a spoon. Spread the breadcrumbs on a plate.
3. Dip the tofu in the flour mixture and coat well in the breadcrumbs.
4. Set the air fryer to 175°C (350°F) for 12 minutes.
5. Lightly mist the air fryer basket with cooking spray and arrange the tofu poppers in it without overlapping. You can lightly mist the poppers again before closing the air fryer.
6. Cook for 10 to 12 minutes or until the tofu poppers are golden brown, turning them halfway through cooking.
7. Remove the tofu poppers onto a plate and let them cool for 5 minutes.

Pair them with coriander cream:
8. While they cool, mix the soured cream and coriander.
9. Serve the tofu poppers with the coriander cream.

# TUNA POPPERS

*Servings: 4*
*Refrigeration Time: 20 mins*

## TOTAL CALORIES:320
Protein: 29.54g | Fats: 7.03g | Carbs: 33.91g

### INGREDIENTS

- 2 (170g / 7 oz) cans tuna in water, drained
- 2 large eggs and 1 egg yolk, lightly beaten
- 170g (¾ cup) breadcrumbs, divided
- 15g (1 tbsp) onion powder
- Salt and black pepper to taste
- Cooking spray

### INSTRUCTIONS

1. In a bowl, combine the tuna, eggs, 110g (½ cup) of breadcrumbs, onion powder, salt, and black pepper. Mix well, cover the bowl, and refrigerate for 20 minutes.
2. Remove the bowl from the refrigerator and mould 30g (2 tbsp) sized balls from the mixture.
3. Mix the breadcrumbs with some salt and black pepper and roll the tuna balls in it until they are well coated.
4. Mist the air fryer basket with cooking spray and arrange the tuna poppers in a single layer.
5. Set the air fryer to 180°C (360°F) for 5 minutes. Fry for 3 to 5 minutes, turning the tuna poppers halfway through cooking until they are golden brown.
6. Remove the tuna poppers onto a serving platter and serve warm.

# VEGGIE PEA BITES

*Servings: 4*
*Refrigeration Time: 30 mins*

## TOTAL CALORIES:340
Protein: 12.24g | Fats: 8.31g | Carbs: 55.87g

### INGREDIENTS

- 1 small cauliflower, cut into small florets
- 4 carrots, roughly chopped
- 1 leek, cleaned and roughly chopped
- 1 small white onion, peeled and diced
- 1 cup garden peas, cooked or canned
- 30g (2 tbsp) all-purpose flour / gluten-free flour or more to thicken
- 5g (1 tsp) grated ginger
- 5g (1 tsp) minced garlic
- 5g (1 tsp) dried coriander
- 5g (1 tsp) cumin powder
- Salt and black pepper to taste
- 15ml (1 tbsp) olive oil
- 2 eggs
- 225g (1 cup) breadcrumbs
- Cooking spray

### INSTRUCTIONS

1. In a food processor, add the cauliflower, carrots, leek, onion, garden peas, flour, ginger, garlic, coriander, cumin, salt, black pepper, and olive oil. Process the ingredients until they break into very small bits. Pour the mixture into a bowl, cover, and refrigerate for 30 minutes.
2. Beat eggs in a bowl.
3. Remove vegetable mixture from the fridge and mould 30g (2 tbsp) sized balls out of it. Dip the balls into the eggs and coat them well in the breadcrumbs.
4. Set the air fryer to 190°C (380°F) for 10 minutes.
5. Lightly mist the air fryer basket with cooking spray and arrange the vegetables balls in it in a single layer. Mist them again with a little cooking spray.
6. Fry the vegetable balls for 10 minutes or until they are golden brown. Meanwhile, turn them after 5 minutes of cooking.
7. Remove the vegetable pea bites to a plate when they are ready. Serve them warm.

# 3 | CROWD PLEASING APPETISERS

*The air fryer seems as though it was created uniquely for appetisers. Creating quick mini bites for visiting guests, whether planned or unexpected, does not have to be stressful. These are some tasty ones I enjoy entertaining with and the air fryer helps make them such an ease.*

## DON'T FORGET TO GET THE **TOP RECIPES** FROM THIS BOOK AS

## A FREE DOWNLOADABLE PDF IN COLOUR

### SCAN THE QR CODE BELOW

*Just follow the steps below to access it via the QR Code (the picture code at the bottom of this page) or click the link if you are reading this on your Phone / Device.*

1. Unlock your phone & open up the phone's camera
2. Make sure you are using the "back" camera (as if you were taking a photo of someone) and point it towards the QR code at the bottom of the page.
3. Tap your phone's screen exactly where the QR code is.
4. A link / pop up will appear. Simply tap that (and make sure you have internet connection) and the FREE PDF containing all of the colored images should appear.

# BACON-WRAPPED ASSORTED MINIS

*Servings: 4*

**TOTAL CALORIES:1166**
Protein: 21.42g | Fats: 97.64g | Carb: 57.34g

## INGREDIENTS

- 16 bacon slices
- 225g (1 cup) dates, seeds removed
- 225g (1 cup) pineapple chunks
- 225g (1 cup) smoked oysters in oil, drained
- 225g (½ lb) scallops
- Toothpicks for holding

## INSTRUCTIONS

1. Slightly stretch each bacon slice and cut each one into halves at their widths.
2. Wrap each date, pineapple, oyster, and scallop with a piece of bacon and secure them with toothpicks. Place them in the air fryer basket in a single layer. You can do them in batches if your frying space is small.
3. Set the air fryer to 200°C (400°F) for 8 minutes. Cook the bacon-wrapped goodies for 3 to 4 minutes on each side or until they are golden brown.
4. Remove the bacon from the air fryer onto a paper towel-lined plate to drain some grease.
5. Serve them with your favourite dipping sauce(s) and enjoy.

# BEEF AND RED WINE RAVIOLI

*Servings: 4*

**TOTAL CALORIES: 422**
Protein: 22.78g | Fats: 14.97g | Carbs: 48.66g

## INGREDIENTS

- 1 (10 oz) package refrigerated beef and red wine ravioli
- 225g (1 cup) breadcrumbs
- 60g (2 oz) pecorino Romano cheese, grated and divided
- 60g (2 oz) Parmigiano-Reggiano cheese, grated and divided
- 7g (1¼ tsp) black pepper, divided
- 3 large eggs
- 15g (1 tbsp) chopped fresh flat-leaf parsley
- Warm marinara sauce for serving

## INSTRUCTIONS

1. Cook the ravioli in a pot of boiling water for 6 minutes or until cooked. Drain the ravioli and place on paper towels to dry.
2. In a bowl, mix the breadcrumbs, half each of the cheeses, and black pepper. Crack the eggs into a bowl and lightly beat them.
3. Dip the ravioli in the eggs and coat them generously with the breadcrumbs and cheese mixture. Place the ravioli in the air fryer basket.
4. Set the air fryer to 175°C (350°F) for 7 minutes.
5. Fry the ravioli for 5 to 7 minutes or until they are golden brown while turning them halfway after cooking.
6. When ready, plate the ravioli and sprinkle on the remaining cheese and parsley.
7. Serve the ravioli with warm marinara sauce.

## 3 BREADED PICKLES WITH DILL MAYO

(IN MINUTES)
PREP **10**
COOK **10**

*Servings: 4*

**TOTAL CALORIES:478**
Protein: 12.63g | Fats: 30.79g | Carbs: 42.19g

### INGREDIENTS

To make the breaded pickles:

- 225g (1 cup) breadcrumbs
- 10g (2 tsp) garlic powder
- 16 jarred (pickled) cucumber spears with dill
- 3 large eggs, beaten
- Cooking spray

To make the dill mayo:
- 120ml (½ cup) mayonnaise, plain flavour
- 15 to 30ml (1 to 2 tbsp) pickle juice
- 45g (3 tbsp) chopped fresh dill

### INSTRUCTIONS

For the breaded pickles:
1. On a plate, mix the breadcrumbs and garlic powder. Dip the cucumber spears into the eggs and coat well with the breadcrumbs.
2. Lightly mist the air fryer basket with cooking spray and arrange the breaded cucumber in it without overlapping.
3. Set the air fryer to 200°C (400°F) for 10 minutes. Bake the breaded cucumber for 5 minutes per side or until they are golden brown.
4. Take out the silicone mould and pop the egg white bites onto a serving plate.
5. Serve warm.

For the dill mayo:
6. In a bowl, mix the mayonnaise, pickle juice, and dill until smooth.
7. Serve the breaded pickles with the dill mayo.

## CHEDDAR AND LEEK TART 4

(IN MINUTES)
PREP **20**
COOK **30**

*Servings: 4*

**TOTAL CALORIES:1162**
Protein: 14.94g | Fats: 95.39g | Carbs: 64.58

### INGREDIENTS

- 30g (1 oz) butter
- 2 medium leeks, sliced
- 5g (1 tsp) caster sugar
- 15g (1 tbsp) chopped fresh thyme
- Salt and black pepper to taste
- 30ml (2 tbsp) double cream
- 450g (17.6 oz) pack refrigerated puff pastry
- 100g (3½ oz) mature Cheddar cheese, grated
- Cooking spray

### INSTRUCTIONS

1. Melt the butter in a skillet over medium heat on a stovetop. Sauté the leeks for 5 minutes or until tender. Stir in the thyme and cook for 1 minute. Then stir in the sugar until it dissolves. Stir in the double cream and season with salt and black pepper. Simmer for 2 minutes and turn the heat off.
2. Roll out the puff pastry and cut out four 15cm rounds. Pinch the edges of each pastry round to create a crust. Spoon the creamed leek onto the pastry, spread out, and top with the cheddar cheese.
3. Set the air fryer to 200°C (400°F) for 20 minutes.
4. Using a flexible spatula, carefully lift two pastries into the air fryer basket and bake for 15 to 20 minutes until they are golden brown and the cheese has melted.
5. Take out the tarts and bake the other two. Serve them warm.

## CHEESE STRAWS CRUSTED IN ROASTED CHICKEN CRISPS

*Servings: 4*

**TOTAL CALORIES: 264**
Protein: 26.09g | Fats: 16.09g | Carbs: 2.84g

### INGREDIENTS

- 1 (150g / 5 oz) bag roast chicken crisps
- 2 eggs, beaten
- 12 mozzarella cheese sticks

### INSTRUCTIONS

1. Line a baking sheet with foil or parchment paper and set it aside.
2. Pour the chicken crisps into a food processor and process until smooth. Spread the crisps on a plate. Also, pour the eggs into a plate for better space to coat the mozzarella sticks.
3. Dip the mozzarella sticks into the eggs on all sides and coat well with the chicken crisps. Lay the cheese sticks on the baking sheet and freeze for 30 minutes.
4. After, set the air fryer to 180°C (390°F) for 8 minutes.
5. Transfer the cheese sticks to the air fryer basket and bake for 3 to 4 minutes per side or until they are golden brown and the cheese is soft. You can do this in batches.
6. Take them out onto a plate and serve them with your favourite dipping sauce.

## CHEESY SWEET POTATO PLATTER

*Servings: 4*

**TOTAL CALORIES: 574**
Protein: 28.34g | Fats: 36.49g | Carbs: 36.79g

### INGREDIENTS

- 6 small (400g) sweet potatoes, peeled and cut into thin wedges
- 20ml (1½ tbsp) olive oil
- 30g (2 tsp) ground cumin
- 15g (1 tsp) paprika
- 3g (½ tsp) sea salt
- 300g (10.5 oz) can red kidney beans in water, drained and rinsed
- 340g (1½ cups) grated smoked cheddar
- 60g (¼ cup) chopped fresh coriander

### INSTRUCTIONS

1. Set the air fryer to 200°C (400°F) for 25 minutes.
2. On a baking tray (one that can fit into your air fryer), spread the potato wedges and drizzle with the olive oil, cumin, paprika, and salt. Mix well to ensure the sweet potatoes are well-coated with the seasoning.
3. Place the tray in the air fryer and bake the potatoes for 20 to 22 minutes or until the sweet potatoes are tender.
4. Spread on the kidney beans and cheddar cheese and bake for 3 more minutes or until the cheese has melted.
5. Take out the tray onto a heat-proof surface and garnish with the coriander. Serve warm.

## COCONUT-CRUSTED SHRIMP WITH SWEET CHILLI VINAIGRETTE

*Servings: 4*

**TOTAL CALORIES: 373**
Protein: 30.4g | Fats: 11.79g | Carbs: 34.91g

### INGREDIENTS

For the coconut-crusted shrimp:
- 450g (1 lb) raw shrimp, peeled and deveined
- 60g (¼ cup) all-purpose flour / gluten-free flour
- 3g (½ tsp) garlic powder
- 3g (½ tsp) salt
- 1g (¼ tsp) black pepper
- 2 large eggs
- 170g (¾ cup) unsweetened shredded coconut
- 60g (¼ cup) panko breadcrumbs

For the sweet chilli vinaigrette:
- 15ml (1 tbsp) sesame oil
- 15ml (1 tbsp) olive oil
- 45ml (3 tbsp) apple cider vinegar
- 45ml (3 tbsp) sweet chilli sauce
- 30ml (2 tbsp) honey
- Salt and black pepper to taste

### INSTRUCTIONS

To make the coconut-crusted shrimp:
1. Using paper towels, pat dry the shrimp.
2. On a plate, mix the flour, garlic powder, salt, and black pepper. Beat eggs, and mix the breadcrumbs and coconut on a plate.
3. Set the air fryer to 180°C (360°F) for 6 minutes.
4. Dredge the shrimp in the flour mixture, then in the eggs, and coat generously with the coconut-breadcrumbs mixture.
5. Mist the air fryer basket with cooking spray and arrange the shrimp in it in a single layer. Mist the shrimp with a little cooking spray.
6. Fry the shrimp for 3 minutes per side or until they are golden brown and crispy.

For the sweet chilli vinaigrette:
7. In a bowl, mix the sesame oil, olive oil, apple cider vinegar, sweet chilli sauce, honey, salt, and black pepper. Mix the ingredients until they are well combined.
8. You can prepare the vinaigrette while the shrimp fries just in time for serving.
9. Serve the ready crusted shrimp with the vinaigrette and have a tasty dip.

## COD AND PEA FRITTERS

*Servings: 4*
*Chilling Time: 30 mins*

**TOTAL CALORIES: 330**
Protein: 21.61g | Fats: 12.93g | Carbs: 31.44g

### INGREDIENTS

- 450g (1 lb) cod fillets
- 450g (1 lb) mashed potatoes, leftover or freshly made
- 5g (1 tsp) butter, at room temperature
- 5 (140 g) bags of frozen peas, defrosted
- 45g (3 tbsp) all-purpose flour / gluten-free flour
- 15ml (1 tbsp) mayonnaise
- 30g (2 tbsp) chopped fresh mint
- 45ml (3 tbsp) rapeseed oil

### INSTRUCTIONS

1. Chop the cod filets into small bits and add them to a bowl. Add the mashed potato, butter, and frozen peas. Using a potato masher, mash the ingredients together until they are smoothly combined. Add the flour, mayonnaise, mint, and rapeseed oil. Mix them until they are well combined.
2. Form eight equal patties from the mixture and place them on a tray. Refrigerate them for 30 minutes.
3. After, set the air fryer to 175°C (350°F) for 6 minutes.
4. Place the patties in the air fryer basket and fry them for 2 to 3 minutes per side or until they are golden brown.
5. Transfer them to a serving platter and serve them with cherry tomatoes and your preferred sauce.

28

## CORIANDER AND MINT TOMATO TARTS

*Servings: 4*

**TOTAL CALORIES:863**
Protein: 8.67g | Fats: 63.22g | Carbs: 67.3g

### INGREDIENTS

- 450g (17.6 oz) pack refrigerated puff pastry
- 30g (2 tbsp) finely chopped fresh coriander
- 30 (2 tbsp) finely chopped fresh mint
- 1 small garlic clove, minced
- A pinch of cayenne pepper
- Salt to taste
- 90ml (6 tbsp) olive oil
- 6 large plum tomatoes, each cut into 4 slices

### INSTRUCTIONS

1. Roll out the puff pastry and cut out four 15cm rounds and place them aside.
2. In a bowl, mix the coriander, mint, garlic, cayenne pepper, salt, and olive oil. Spread half of this mixture on the puff pastry rounds.
3. Divide the tomato slices on the pastry and spread the remaining herb oil on them.
4. Set the air fryer to 200°C (400°F) for 20 minutes.
5. Place two pastries in the air fryer basket and bake for 15 to 20 minutes or until the pastry is golden brown and the tomatoes tender.
6. Take out the tarts and bake the other two.
7. Serve the tomato tarts warm.

## CORN AND HALLOUMI WITH LEMON BUTTER

*Servings: 4*

**TOTAL CALORIES:395**
Protein: 11.16g | Fats: 36.94g | Carbs: 5.88g

### INGREDIENTS

- 8 oz block halloumi cheese
- 120ml (½ cup) melted butter
- ½ lemon, juiced
- 3g (½ tsp) chopped fresh thyme
- 110g (½ cup) canned sweet corn in water, drained

### INSTRUCTIONS

1. Slice the halloumi into 2cm slabs and lay them in the air fryer basket.
2. Set the air fryer to 180°C (390°F) for 6 minutes. Bake the halloumi for 2 to 3 minutes per side or until they are golden brown.
3. Meanwhile, in a bowl, mix the butter, lemon juice, and thyme.
4. Transfer the halloumi to a platter when ready and spoon some of the sweet corn on top. Drizzle the lemon butter all over to your taste and serve.

## COTTAGE CHEESE-STUFFED PEPPERS

*Servings: 4*

**TOTAL CALORIES:282**
Protein: 17.94g | Fats: 17.46g | Carbs: 15.36g

### INGREDIENTS

- 12 sweet baby peppers, any colour of choice
- 10ml (2 tsp) olive oil
- 250g (8 oz) package soft cheese, at room temperature
- 150g (2/3 cup) cottage cheese
- 2 stalks salad onions, finely chopped
- 3g (½ tsp) garlic powder
- 3g (½ tsp) salt
- 5ml (1 tsp) hot sauce or to taste, also optional

### INSTRUCTIONS

1. Cut the peppers lengthwise into halves and clean out their seeds and membranes. Place the peppers on a plate and drizzle them with olive oil.
2. In a bowl, mix the soft cheese, cottage cheese, salad onions, garlic powder, salt, and hot sauce, if using. When the mixture is well combined, spoon it into the peppers and level their tops with the back of the spoon.
3. Set the air fryer to 180°C (360°F) for 8 minutes.
4. Set the peppers in the air fryer basket and bake for 6 to 8 minutes or until they are golden brown on top and tender. You can do them in batches.
5. Put the peppers on a plate and serve them warm.

## CREAMY BACON, CHERRY, AND BLUE CHEESE-STUFFED MUSHROOMS

*Servings: 4*

**TOTAL CALORIES:336**
Protein: 16.14g | Fats: 221g | Carbs: 23.1g

### INGREDIENTS

- 4 bacon slices
- 4 medium portabella mushrooms
- 110g (4 oz) soft cheese, at room temperature
- 60g (¼ cup) small diced shallot
- 60g (4 oz) blue cheese, crumbled
- 5g (1 tsp) finely chopped fresh thyme
- 75g (1/3 cup) small diced dried cherries
- 1g (¼ tsp) black pepper
- 30g (2 tbsp) dried breadcrumbs
- Chopped fresh thyme for garnish

### INSTRUCTIONS

1. Set the air fryer to 175°C (350°F) for 5 minutes.
2. Lay the bacon slices in the air fryer basket and cook for 4 to 5 minutes or until the bacon is golden brown and crispy.
3. Clean up the mushrooms by removing their stems and gills. Wash them clean and pat them dry with paper towels.
4. When the bacon pieces are ready, take them out and place them on paper towels to drain grease and cool. After, chop them into small pieces and add them to a bowl.
5. In this bowl, add the soft cheese, shallot, blue cheese, thyme, cherries, and black pepper. Mix the ingredients well.
6. Spoon the creamy bacon mixture into the mushrooms and sprinkle the breadcrumbs on top.
7. Place the mushrooms in the air fryer basket (you don't need to clean out the bacon grease as it will add flavour to the mushrooms) and cook the mushrooms at 175°C (350°F) for 6 minutes or until the mushrooms are tender but hold their shapes.
8. Plate the stuffed mushrooms, garnish with thyme, and serve them warm.

# FRIED GREEN TOMATOES WITH SWEET CORN AND CRAB STACKS

*Servings: 4*

**TOTAL CALORIES:1284**
Protein: 25.35g | Fats: 30.69g |
Carbs: 215.29g

# GUINNESS-BATTERED ONION RINGS

*Servings: 4*

**TOTAL CALORIES:368**
Protein: 8.91g | Fats: 7.14g |
Carbs: 68.2g

## INGREDIENTS

**For the fried green tomatoes:**
- 2 to 3 large green tomatoes
- 450g (2 cups) all-purpose flour
- 3g (½ tsp) dry mustard
- A pinch of cayenne pepper
- Salt and black pepper to taste
- 2 large eggs
- 420ml (1¾) cups milk
- 225g (1 cup) cornmeal
- 450g (2 cups) panko breadcrumbs
- Cooking spray

**For the sweet corn and crab salad:**
- 1 (160g / ¾ cup) can sweet corn in water, drained
- 2 (110g / ½ cup) packs lump crabmeat
- 1 lime, juiced
- 1 small shallot, minced
- 110g (½ cup) chopped fresh coriander
- Salt and black pepper to taste
- 15ml (1 tbsp) olive oil

## INSTRUCTIONS

**For the fried green tomatoes:**
1. Slice the green tomatoes into rounds and pat them dry with paper towels.
2. On a plate, mix the flour, mustard, cayenne pepper, salt, and black pepper. Whisk eggs with milk. On a plate, mix the cornmeal and breadcrumbs.
3. Dredge each tomato round in the flour mixture, then in the eggs, and then coat generously with the cornmeal mixture.
4. Set the air fryer to 175°C (350°F) for 6 mins.
5. Mist the air fryer basket with cooking spray and lay the coated green tomatoes in it in a single layer.
6. Fry for 2 to 3 minutes per side or until they are golden brown.
7. When they are ready, transfer them to a wire rack to cool.

**For the sweet corn and crab salad:**
8. In a bowl, mix the sweet corn, crabmeat, lime juice, shallot, coriander, salt, black pepper, and olive oil. Mix well.
9. Spoon the salad on the fried green tomatoes and serve.

## INGREDIENTS

**For the Guinness-battered onion rings:**
- 225g (1 cup) all-purpose flour / gluten-free flour
- 4g (¾ tsp) baking soda
- Salt and black pepper to taste
- 1 egg, lightly beaten
- 240ml (1 cup) Guinness
- 2 to 3 sweet onions, peeled, sliced into rings, and separated
- Cooking spray

**For the serving sauce:**
- 120ml (½ cup) mayonnaise
- 120ml (½ cup) ketchup

## INSTRUCTIONS

**For the Guinness-battered onion rings:**
1. In a bowl, mix the flour, baking soda, salt, and black pepper until smooth. Add the egg and Guinness then whisk until smooth.
2. Lightly mist the air fryer basket with cooking spray. Dip the onion rings into the Guinness batter and place them in the air fryer basket in a single layer. Lightly mist again with cooking spray.
3. Set the air fryer to 190°C (375°F) for 4 minutes.
4. Fry the onion rings for 1 to 2 minutes per side or until golden brown.
5. Take out the onion rings.

**For the serving sauce:**
6. In a bowl, mix the mayonnaise and ketchup until smooth and pale pink.
7. Serve the onion rings with the sauce.

## PORK SAUSAGE ROLLS

*Servings: 4*

(IN MINUTES)
PREP
10
COOK
12

### TOTAL CALORIES: 376
Protein: 26.33g | Fats: 18.45g | Carbs: 26.43g

### INGREDIENTS

- 450g (1 lb) pork sausages
- 30ml (2 tbsp) tomato sauce
- 2 eggs, cracked into a bowl, divided
- 110g (½ cup) breadcrumbs
- 2 sheets puff pastry, defrosted
- Sesame seeds, to garnish

### INSTRUCTIONS

1. Remove the meat from the sausage casings into a bowl. Add the tomato sauce, one egg, and breadcrumbs. Mix well.
2. Lay out the puff pastry sheets onto a clean flat surface and spread the sausage mixture on top, leaving about 1cm space along their longer edges for sealing. Roll the pastry over the filling and seal at the end. Whisk the other egg and brush on the pastry. Sprinkle the sesame seeds on top.
3. Cut each pastry into 6 pieces and lay them in the air fryer basket in a single layer.
4. Set the air fryer to 200°C (400°F) for 12 minutes and bake the pastry rolls for 10 to 12 minutes or until they are golden brown.
5. Transfer them to a wire rack to cool and serve them with tomato sauce.

## SCOTTISH TATTIE SCONES WITH SMOKED SALMON

*Servings: 4*

(IN MINUTES)
PREP
35
COOK
6

### TOTAL CALORIES: 464
Protein: 13.79g | Fats: 17.18g | Carbs: 63.33g

### INGREDIENTS

- 450g (1 lb) potatoes, peeled and cut into 3-5cm chunks
- 3g (½ tsp) salt or to taste
- 225g (1 cup) all-purpose flour / gluten-free flour, plus extra for dusting
- 45g (3 tbsp) butter
- 30g (2 tbsp) double cream
- Cooking spray
- 45g (3 tbsp) British creme fraiche
- 100g (3.5 oz) smoked salmon
- Chive snippings to garnish

### INSTRUCTIONS

1. Boil the potatoes in a pot of water for 15 to 20 minutes or until they are tender. Drain the potatoes and pour them into a bowl.
2. Season the potatoes with salt and mash until smooth. Add the flour and butter and mix until smooth. Add the double cream and stir until smooth and creamed.
3. Form 5cm size balls from the mixture and place on a floured surface. Roll each ball into a round pancake shape and prick all over with a fork.
4. Set the air fryer to 190°C (380°F) for 6 minutes.
5. Mist the air fryer basket with cooking spray and lay some of the scones in the basket in a single layer. Cook for 2 to 3 minutes per side or until the scones are golden brown per side.
6. Transfer the scones to a platter and make more.
7. Add dollops of creme fraiche on each scone, spread on the smoked salmon, and garnish with the chive snippings.

## SEARED SCALLOPS WITH POMEGRANATE GLAZE

Servings: 4

### TOTAL CALORIES: 226
Protein: 6.57g | Fats: 1.9g | Carbs: 16.62g

### INGREDIENTS
- 120ml (½ cup) pomegranate juice, divided
- 15ml (1 tbsp) aged balsamic vinegar
- 30ml (2 tbsp) gluten-free tamari sauce
- 680g (1½ lb) large sea scallops
- Salt and black pepper to taste
- Cooking spray
- 225g (1 cup) baby rocket for serving
- Pomegranate arils for garnish

### INSTRUCTIONS
1. In a pot, mix the pomegranate juice, balsamic vinegar, and tamari sauce. Place the pot over medium heat on a stovetop. Once boiling, reduce the heat to low and simmer until the sauce reduces by half and thickens. Turn the heat off and set aside.
2. Set the air fryer to 200°C (400°F) for 4 minutes.
3. Season the scallops on both sides with salt and black pepper.
4. Mist the air fryer basket with cooking spray and place in the scallops without overlapping. Cook them for 2 minutes per side or until they are golden brown.
5. Meanwhile, create a serving bed with the rocket and arrange the scallops on top. Drizzle on the pomegranate glaze and garnish with the pomegranate arils.

## SPICY RASPBERRY WINGS WITH WORCESTERSHIRE

Servings: 4

### TOTAL CALORIES: 786
Protein: 100.22g | Fats: 22.24g | Carbs: 41.95g

### INGREDIENTS
- 5ml (1 tsp) olive oil
- 340g (1½ cups) fresh raspberries
- 90g (6 tbsp) brown sugar
- 30ml (2 tbsp) fresh lemon juice
- 30ml (2 tbsp) Worcestershire sauce
- 15ml (1 tbsp) molasses
- 30ml (2 tbsp) ketchup
- 5ml (1 tsp) onion powder
- 5ml (1 tsp) garlic powder
- 10ml (2 tsp) mustard
- 1ml to 3ml (¼ to ½ tsp) hot sauce
- 1.8 kg (4 lb) chicken wings, separated at their joints
- Salt to taste
- Chopped fresh parsley for garnish

### INSTRUCTIONS
1. In a food processor, combine the olive oil, raspberries, brown sugar, and lemon juice. Blend the mixture until smooth.
2. Pour the mixture into a pot and stir in the Worcestershire sauce, molasses, ketchup, onion and garlic powder, mustard, and salt. Stir well and cook over low heat on a stovetop for 10 minutes or until thickened. Set aside.
3. Pat dry the chicken with paper towels and season with salt.
4. Mist the air fryer basket with cooking spray and add the chicken to the basket.
5. Set the air fryer to 200°C (400°F) for 16 minutes. Fry the chicken for 8 minutes per side or until they are golden brown and cooked within.
6. Remove the chicken into the bowl and add about ½ cup of the raspberry sauce to them. Mix to coat well and plate.
7. Garnish with parsley and serve.

## SPINACH AND FETA STUFFED MUSHROOMS

*Servings: 4*

**TOTAL CALORIES:384**
Protein: 25.52g | Fats: 26.66g | Carbs: 13.57g

### INGREDIENTS

- 16 small white mushrooms
- 15ml (1 tbsp) olive oil
- 2 salad onions, chopped
- 2 garlic cloves, minced
- 450g (2 cups) packed chopped baby spinach
- 45g (3 tbsp) chopped fresh parsley
- 110g (4 oz) soft cheese, at room temperature
- ½ block feta cheese, crumbled
- Salt and black pepper to taste
- 170g (¾ cup) shredded mozzarella cheese
- Chopped fresh parsley for garnish

### INSTRUCTIONS

1. Clean out the stems of the mushrooms, rinse them, and pat them dry with paper towels. Set them aside.
2. Heat the olive oil in a skillet over medium heat on a stove top. Sauté the salad onions for 2 minutes and stir in the garlic. Cook for 1 minute and add the spinach and parsley. Cook them for 3 minutes or until the spinach starts wilting. Stir in the soft cheese, feta cheese, and season with salt and black pepper until the soft cheese melts.
3. Spoon the mixture into the mushrooms and cover their tops with mozzarella cheese.
4. Set the air fryer to 200°C (400°F) for 20 minutes.
5. Set the mushrooms in the air fryer basket with the cheese side facing upwards and bake for 18 to 20 minutes or until the mushrooms are tender.
6. Remove the mushrooms onto a serving platter and garnish with parsley.

## WELSH RAREBIT STICKS

*Servings: 4*

**TOTAL CALORIES:318**
Protein: 4.87g | Fats: 3.3g | Carbs: 66.91g

### INGREDIENTS

- 4 bread slices, type of choice
- 1 egg yolk
- 15ml (1 tbsp) milk
- 60g (¼ cup) grated light matured cheddar cheese
- Tomato jam for serving

### INSTRUCTIONS

1. Cut the bread slices into 3cm thick sticks and place them aside.
2. Set the air fryer to 175°C (350°F) for 4 minutes.
3. In a bowl, whisk the egg yolk, milk, and 40g of cheddar cheese. Spread the mixture on both sides of the breadsticks and top with the remaining cheese.
4. Lightly grease the air fryer basket with cooking spray and place the coated bread sticks in it. Toast the bread pieces for 2 minutes per side or until the cheese melts.
5. Take out the breadsticks and serve with tomato jam.

# 4 | QUICK-FIXES FOR BREAKFAST & BRUNCH

*Breakfast and brunch bring delightful sparks. By simply playing with the colours of vegetables, you can always create a good feeling early in the day. These recipes aren't short of being delicious and are intentionally made to excite you, not just satisfy you.*

## DON'T FORGET TO GET THE

## **TOP RECIPES** FROM THIS BOOK AS

## **A FREE DOWNLOADABLE PDF IN COLOUR**

**SCAN THE QR CODE BELOW**

*Just follow the steps below to access it via the QR Code (the picture code at the bottom of this page) or click the link if you are reading this on your Phone / Device.*

1. Unlock your phone & open up the phone's camera
2. Make sure you are using the "back" camera (as if you were taking a photo of someone) and point it towards the QR code at the bottom of the page.
3. Tap your phone's screen exactly where the QR code is.
4. A link / pop up will appear. Simply tap that (and make sure you have internet connection) and the FREE PDF containing all of the colored images should appear.

## BLUEBERRY MUFFINS

*Servings: 4*

(IN MINUTES)
PREP 10
COOK 13

### TOTAL CALORIES: 631
Protein: 11.67g | Fats: 19.08g | Carbs: 103.67g

### INGREDIENTS

- 1 large egg
- 75g (2/3 cup) whole milk
- 60g (¼ cup) canola oil
- 110g (½ cup) granulated sugar
- 340g (1½ cups) all-purpose flour / gluten-free flour
- 10g (2 tsp) baking powder
- 3g (½ tsp) fine sea salt
- 225g (1 cup) fresh blueberries plus extra for the top's burst

### INSTRUCTIONS

1. Grease 4 to 6 silicone muffin cups with cooking spray and set them aside.
2. Crack the egg into a bowl and whisk with the milk and canola oil until smooth. Add the sugar and whisk until smooth. Pour in the flour, baking powder, and salt. Whisk until smooth batter forms and fold in the blueberries.
3. Pour the batter into the muffin cups and top them with 2 to 3 blueberries per cup. Place the cups in the air fryer basket.
4. Set the air fryer to 170°C (340°F) for 13 minutes.
5. Bake the muffins for 13 minutes or until they are set by performing the toothpick test.
6. Take the muffins out and let them cool for 10 minutes in the cups. After, pop them out of the cups and place them on a wire rack to cool. Enjoy them.

## BREAKFAST STUFFED SCONES

*Servings: 4*

(IN MINUTES)
PREP 10
COOK 5

### TOTAL CALORIES: 478
Protein: 20.97g | Fats: 34.59g | Carbs: 20.04g

### INGREDIENTS

- 225g (1 cup) scrambled eggs
- 110g (½ cup) cooked crumbled bacon
- 110g (½ cup) shredded cheddar cheese
- 4 refrigerated all-butter scones
- 15ml (1 tbsp) melted butter

### INSTRUCTIONS

1. In a bowl, mix the eggs, bacon, and cheddar cheese.
2. Create a pocket through the side of each scone and stuff in the egg mixture. After, brush the top of the scones with butter.
3. Set the air fryer to 160°C (320°F) for 5 minutes.
4. Arrange the scones in the air fryer basket and bake for 3 to 5 minutes or until the scones are golden brown.
5. Serve the stuffed scones warm.

## CHEESE AND TUNA AVOCADO BOATS

*Servings: 4*

**TOTAL CALORIES:513**
Protein: 32.18g | Fats: 38.53g | Carbs: 12.49g

### INGREDIENTS

- 2 (110g) cans tuna in oil, drained
- 225g (1 cup) shredded cheddar cheese, divided
- 1 tomato, diced
- ½ red onion, diced
- 5g (1 tsp) chopped fresh dill or cilantro
- Salt and black pepper to taste
- 2 medium avocados, cut in halves and pits removed

### INSTRUCTIONS

1. In a bowl, mix the tuna, half of the cheddar cheese, tomato, onion, dill or cilantro, salt, and black pepper. Mix well and spoon the mixture into the avocados. Spread the remaining cheddar cheese on the avocados and carefully place them in the air fryer basket.
2. Set the air fryer to 180°C (360°F) for 4 minutes.
3. Bake the avocados for 3 to 4 minutes or until the cheese has melted.
4. Place the avocados on serving plates and serve warm.

## CHIVE AND CHEDDAR SCRAMBLED EGGS

*Servings: 4*

**TOTAL CALORIES:308**
Protein: 19.44g | Fats: 23.07g | Carbs: 5.2g

### INGREDIENTS

- 8 eggs
- 60ml (4 tbsp) double cream
- Salt and black pepper to taste
- 110g (½ cup) Red Leicester cheese, finely grated
- 30g (2 tbsp) chopped fresh chives plus extra for garnish
- 8ml (½ tbsp) softened butter

### INSTRUCTIONS

1. Crack the eggs into a bowl and whisk with the double cream, salt, and black pepper until smooth. Add half of the cheese and chives and mix well.
2. Brush a dish (air fryer friendly) with butter and pour in the egg mixture. Cover the dish with foil and place in the air fryer basket.
3. Set the air fryer to 175°C (350°F) for 12 minutes.
4. Cook the eggs for 8 to 12 minutes while stirring every 3 to 4 minutes or until they are soft and set.
5. Take out the eggs, take off the foil and garnish with the remaining cheese and some chives. Serve warm with some muffins or breakfast platter.

# CLASSIC ENGLISH BREAKFAST

*Servings: 4+*

(IN MINUTES)
PREP 10
COOK 15

**TOTAL CALORIES: 469**
Protein: 24.8g | Fats: 19.88g | Carbs: 48.49g

## INGREDIENTS

- 4 eggs
- Salt and black pepper to taste
- 4 hashbrowns
- 12 small mushrooms
- 4 sausages
- 4 tomatoes, sliced
- 4 bacon slices
- 225g (1 cup) baked beans

## INSTRUCTIONS

1. Set the air fryer to 180°C (360°F) for 15 minutes.
2. Crack the eggs into 4 small ramekins, season them with salt and black pepper, and set them aside.
3. Place the hashbrowns and mushrooms in the air fryer basket and start cooking.
4. When they have cooked for 3 minutes, open the air fryer and add the sausages.
5. When they have cooked for 1 minute, add the tomatoes.
6. Cook for 1 minute and add the bacon.
7. After cooking for 3 minutes, add the eggs and cook for 5 to 7 minutes or until the eggs set to your likeness.
8. Meanwhile, pour the baked beans into 4 small ramekins.
9. When the eggs are ready, take them out and place in the baked beans. Continue cooking for 3 to 5 minutes or until the baked beans warm through.
10. Remove all the elements and share them into 4 serving plates.
11. Serve immediately.

# DROP SCONES

*Servings: 4*

(IN MINUTES)
PREP 10
COOK 8

**TOTAL CALORIES: 325**
Protein: 9.61g | Fats: 4.06g | Carbs: 61.72g

## INGREDIENTS

- 225g (1 cup) all-purpose flour / gluten-free flour
- 3g (½ tbsp) baking powder
- 60g (¼ cup) golden caster sugar
- 2g (½ tsp) fine salt
- 1 large egg, beaten
- 300ml (1¼ cup) milk
- Cooking spray

For serving:

- Butter
- Maple syrup
- Fresh fruits of choice

## INSTRUCTIONS

1. In a bowl, mix the flour, baking powder, sugar, and salt. Whisk the egg and milk until smooth and combine with the flour mixture until smooth batter forms.
2. Grease 4 (15cm) pie tins with cooking spray and equally divide the batter into the tins. Using a tablespoon or butter knife, spread the batter to the sides of the tins to ensure even levelling.
3. Set the air fryer to 200°C (400°F) for 8 minutes.
4. Place two tins in the air fryer basket and bake for 7 to 8 minutes or until they are golden brown and set within.
5. Transfer the tins to a platter and bake the other two.
6. Remove the pancakes onto serving plates. Top with butter, maple syrup, and fresh fruits.

*THE UK AIR FRYER COOKBOOK*

## EGG AND TURKEY ROLLS

*Servings: 4*

**TOTAL CALORIES: 451**
Protein: 21.11g | Fats: 14.2g | Carbs: 62.94g

### INGREDIENTS

- 225g (1 cup) leftover turkey, finely chopped
- 225g (1 cup) sausage stuffing mix
- 110g (½ cup) scrambled eggs
- 12 small whole-wheat or gluten-free wraps
- 15ml (1 tbsp) melted butter

### INSTRUCTIONS

1. In a bowl, mix the turkey, sausage stuffing mix, and eggs.
2. Lay out the wraps and top their centres with the turkey mixture. Roll the wraps over the filling. Brush them with the melted butter.
3. Set the air fryer to 190°C (380°F) for 5 minutes.
4. Lay the wraps in the air fryer basket and cook for 3 to 5 minutes or until they are golden brown.
5. Take them out, slice, and serve.

## FLAXSEED TOASTS WITH STRAWBERRIES AND MAPLE SYRUP

*Servings: 4*

**TOTAL CALORIES: 334**
Protein: 10.56g | Fats: 11.61g | Carbs: 49.04g

### INGREDIENTS

- 4 (1½ oz) whole-grain or gluten-free bread slices
- 2 large eggs
- 60g (¼ cup) milk
- 3g (½ tsp) ground cinnamon
- 5g (1 tsp) vanilla extract
- 60g (¼ cup) packed light brown sugar, divided
- 75g (2/3 cup) flaxseed meal
- Cooking spray

For serving:
- 2 cups fresh strawberries, hulled and sliced
- 8 tsp pure maple syrup, divided
- 1 tsp powdered sugar

### INSTRUCTIONS

1. For your preferred presentation, you may cut the bread into diagonal triangles, sticks, or leave them whole. Set them aside.
2. Crack the eggs into a wide bowl and whisk with the milk, cinnamon, and vanilla until smooth. On a plate, mix the flaxseed meal and brown sugar until smooth.
3. Dip the bread pieces on both sides in the egg mixture and let them soak for a few seconds. Transfer the bread to the flaxseed meal and coat well on both sides.
4. Set the air fryer to 190°C (375°F) for 10 minutes.
5. Mist the air fryer basket with cooking spray and lay in the bread pieces without overlapping. Bake for 4 to 5 minutes per side or until they are golden brown.
6. Plate the toasts, top with some strawberries, drizzle with maple syrup, and dust with powdered sugar.

## HAM AND BROCCOLI EGG MUFFINS

*Servings: 4*

### TOTAL CALORIES: 234
Protein: 18.47g | Fats: 14.29g | Carbs: 8.73g

### INGREDIENTS
- 5 eggs
- Salt and black pepper to taste
- 30ml (2 tbsp) double cream
- 4 slices ham, chopped
- ½ bunch of broccoli, cut into small florets
- 1 garlic clove, minced
- 75g (1/3 cup) grated mild cheese of choice
- A pinch of red chilli flakes

### INSTRUCTIONS
1. Crack the eggs into a bowl, season with a little salt and black pepper, and whisk with the double cream.
2. In 4 ramekins, divide the ham, broccoli, garlic, cheese, and red chilli flakes. Mix well and pour the eggs over.
3. Set the air fryer to 180°C (360°F) for 15 minutes.
4. Set the ramekins in the air fryer basket and bake for 10 to 15 minutes or until the eggs are set within.
5. Transfer the ramekins to a heat-proof surface and let them cool slightly.

## HOT HAM AND CHEESE WRAPS

*Servings: 4*

### TOTAL CALORIES: 326
Protein: 17.27g | Fats: 20.81 8g | Carbs: 18.43g

### INGREDIENTS
- 4 large whole-wheat or gluten-free wraps
- 20ml (4 tsp) Dijon mustard
- 30ml (2 tbsp) mayonnaise
- 8 slices honey roast ham
- 15ml (1 tbsp) butter, melted
- 4 slices Swiss cheese

### INSTRUCTIONS
1. Lay out the tortillas on a flat surface and spread the mustard and mayonnaise on them. Lay on two ham pieces on each and top with one cheese slice. Tightly roll up the wraps over the filling and brush with melted butter.
2. Set the air fryer to 190°C (380°F) for 5 minutes.
3. Place the wraps in the air fryer basket and cook for 5 minutes or until they are golden brown. You can check them after 3 minutes of cooking for your desired colour. Cook them for up to 5 minutes.
4. Take out the wraps onto a plate, slice, and serve them warm.

## LOADED POTATO SKINS

*Servings: 4*

**TOTAL CALORIES: 1081**
Protein: 43.06g | Fats: 70.84g | Carbs: 69.71g

### INGREDIENTS

- 4 large yellow potatoes, well-scrubbed
- 15ml (1 tbsp) olive oil
- Salt and black pepper to taste
- 12 bacon slices
- 225g (1 cup) shredded cheddar cheese
- 225g (1 cup) shredded Red Leicester cheese
- ½ cup soured cream plus more for serving
- 15g (1 tbsp) chopped fresh chives for garnish

### INSTRUCTIONS

1. Set the air fryer to 200°C (400°F) for 30 minutes.
2. Using a fork, pierce holes all around the potatoes. Rub with the olive oil and season with salt and black pepper.
3. Place the potatoes in the air fryer basket and bake for 30 minutes or until the potatoes are tender and their skins still in good shape. After 20 minutes of cooking the potatoes, add the bacon to the basket and cook until they are golden brown.
4. Take out the potatoes and bacon. Let potatoes cool, and chop the bacon.
5. Cut potatoes in halves lengthwise and scoop out their flesh into a bowl. Set the skins on a plate with the scooped side facing upwards.
6. In the potato flesh bowl, add half each of the bacon and cheeses, and all of the soured cream. Mix until the potatoes are creamy.
7. Spoon the mixture into the potato skins and top with the remaining cheeses.
8. Place them in the air fryer basket and bake at 196°C (385°F) for 10 minutes or until the cheeses melt.
9. Take them out and top with some soured cream, remaining bacon, and chives.

## MUSHROOM AND SAUSAGE BREAKFAST CASSEROLE

*Servings: 4*

**TOTAL CALORIES: 1006**
Protein: 33.61g | Fats: 93.64g | Carbs: 8.82g

### INGREDIENTS

- 4 large eggs
- 30ml (2 tbsp) double cream
- 2g (½ tsp) dried chives or parsley
- Salt and black pepper to taste
- 225g (1 cup) cooked mushrooms, sliced or chopped
- 450g (1 lb) breakfast sausage, pre-cooked
- 225g (1 cup) diced tomatoes
- 110g (½ cup) shredded cheddar cheese

### INSTRUCTIONS

1. Crack the eggs into a bowl and whisk with the double cream until smooth. Season with the chives or parsley, salt, and black pepper. Mix and set it aside.
2. Grease 4 small ramekins with cooking spray and divide the mushrooms, sausage, and tomatoes in them. Pour in the egg mixture and top with the cheddar cheese.
3. Set the air fryer to 170°C (340°F) for 8 minutes.
4. Place the ramekins in the air fryer and bake for 5 to 8 minutes or until the cheese melts and the casserole sets within.
5. Carefully remove the ramekins onto serving plates and serve warm.

## NUT, RAISINS, AND CHOCOLATE COOKIES

Servings: 4

**TOTAL CALORIES: 1042**
Protein: 20.46g | Fats: 47.63g | Carbs: 138.95g

### INGREDIENTS

- 110g (½ cup) unsalted butter, melted
- 60g (¼ cup) white sugar
- 110g (½ cup) brown sugar
- 1 egg, at room temperature, cracked into a bowl
- 5ml (1 tsp) vanilla extract
- 340g (1½ cups) all-purpose flour / gluten-free flour
- 5g (1 tsp) baking soda
- 1g (¼ tsp) salt
- 110g (½ cup) semi-sweet chocolate chips
- 60g (¼ cup) raisins
- 60g (¼ cup) chopped hazelnuts or your preferred nut or seed substitute

### INSTRUCTIONS

1. In a bowl, mix the butter, white and brown sugar, egg, and vanilla until smooth. In another bowl, mix the flour, baking soda, and salt. Combine both mixtures until smooth and fold in the chocolate chips, raisins, and nuts (or seeds). Cover the bowl and refrigerate for 30 minutes to 1 hour. Overnight refrigeration is also fine.
2. Set the air fryer to 162°C (325°F) for 7 minutes.
3. Line the air fryer basket with parchment paper. Scoop 30g (2 tbsp) sized dough balls onto the parchment paper with 3cm spacing between each. You should fit 2 to 4 dough pieces in the air fryer basket.
4. Bake for 5 to 7 minutes or until the cookies are golden brown and set.
5. Transfer the cookies to a wire rack to cool.
6. Serve them with cold or warm milk.

## PEPPERS AND POTATOES

Servings: 4

**TOTAL CALORIES: 223**
Protein: 4.71g | Fats: 7.12g | Carbs: 36.72g

### INGREDIENTS

- 340 (1½ lb) baby gold potatoes, peeled and cut into large dices
- 1 large red pepper, seeded and diced
- 1 large green pepper, seeded and diced
- 30ml (2 tbsp) olive oil
- 5g (1 tsp) onion powder
- 10g (2 tsp) garlic powder
- Salt and black pepper to taste

### INSTRUCTIONS

1. In a bowl, add the potatoes, peppers, olive oil, onion powder, garlic powder, salt, and black pepper. Toss the ingredients until well-coated.
2. Set the air fryer to 200°C (400°F) for 35 minutes.
3. Spoon the potatoes and peppers into the air fryer basket and bake for 30 to 35 minutes or until golden brown and the potatoes are tender. Meanwhile, shake the basket every 10 minutes.
4. When ready, spoon the potatoes and peppers into a platter and serve warm.

## RASPBERRY TOAST CUPS

*Servings: 4*

**TOTAL CALORIES: 549**
Protein: 17.9g | Fats: 14.94g |
Carbs: 89.58g

### INGREDIENTS

For the toasts:
- 4 bread slices, cut into 1cm cubes
- 225g (1 cup) fresh or frozen raspberries
- 110g (4 oz) soft cheese, cold and cut into (1cm / ½-inch) cubes
- 4 large eggs
- 240ml (1 cup) milk
- 15ml (1 tbsp) maple syrup

For the raspberry syrup:
- 10g (2 tsp) corn starch
- 80ml (2/3 cup) water
- 450g (2 cups) fresh or frozen raspberries, divided
- 3g (½ tsp) grated lemon zest
- 15ml (1 tbsp) lemon juice
- 15ml (1 tbsp) maple syrup

### INSTRUCTIONS

For the toasts:
1. Divide half of the bread into four medium ramekins and top with half each of the raspberries and soft cheese. Repeat the layering process a second time the same way.
2. Crack the eggs into a bowl and whisk with the milk and maple syrup. Pour the mixture evenly over the raspberries and bread layers. Cover each ramekin with foil and refrigerate for 1 hour.
3. Set the air fryer to 163°C (325°F) for 15 minutes.
4. Uncover the ramekins, place them in the air fryer, and bake for 12 to 15 minutes or until the toasts are set.

For the raspberry syrup:
5. In a small saucepan, mix the corn starch and water until smooth. Add 1½ cups raspberries, lemon zest, lemon juice, and maple syrup. Bring to a boil and then reduce the heat to low and simmer for 4 to 5 minutes or until the syrup has thickened.
6. Strain the syrup and mix in the remaining raspberries.
7. Take out the ramekins, drizzle on the raspberry syrup, and serve warm.

## SIMPLE BRUNCH PEPPERS

*Servings: 4*

**TOTAL CALORIES: 158**
Protein: 12.5g | Fats: 9.36g |
Carbs: 5.3g

### INGREDIENTS

- 2 large sweet or bell peppers, colour of choice
- 2 tsp olive oil
- Salt and black pepper to taste
- 110g (½ cup) turkey mince, pre-cooked
- 4 large eggs
- A pinch of red chilli flakes, optional

### INSTRUCTIONS

1. Cut the peppers in halves lengthwise and clean out the seeds and membranes. Season them with olive oil, salt, and black pepper.
2. Spoon the turkey into the peppers and crack an egg into each pepper. Season lightly with salt and black pepper and sprinkle with some red chilli flakes if using.
3. Set the air fryer to 198°C (390°F) for 13 minutes.
4. Carefully set the peppers in the air fryer basket and bake for 10 to 13 minutes or until the eggs are set to your desire.
5. Take out the peppers, garnish with some parsley and serve warm.

## SPINACH, EGG, AND FETA CUPS

*Servings: 4*

**TOTAL CALORIES: 219**
Protein: 11.96g | Fats: 16.21g
| Carbs: 9.05g

### INGREDIENTS

- 2 tsp extra virgin olive oil, divide
- 280g (10 oz) frozen spinach, defrosted
- Salt and black pepper to taste
- 50g (1.8 oz) crumbled feta cheese
- 4 large eggs
Serving options:
- Sliced avocados
- Diced or halved tomatoes
- Fresh herbs

### INSTRUCTIONS

1. Grease four ramekins with 15ml (1 tbsp) with olive oil.
2. Divide the spinach between the ramekins and season with salt and black pepper. Spread the feta cheese around the spinach while creating a hole at the centre for the eggs. Crack an egg into each hole, drizzle with the remaining olive oil and season with salt and black pepper.
3. Set the air fryer to 200°C (400°F) for 7 minutes.
4. Set the ramekins in the air fryer basket and bake for 5 to 7 minutes or until the eggs are set to your likeness.
5. Take out the ramekins and serve with some avocados, tomatoes, and herbs as preferred.

## THYME SAUSAGE PATTIES

*Servings: 4*

**TOTAL CALORIES: 341**
Protein: 29.29g | Fats: 23.62g |
Carbs: 0.75g

### INGREDIENTS

- 450g (1lb) pork mince
- Salt and black pepper to taste
- 1g (⅛ tsp) dried thyme
- 3g (½ tsp) fennel seeds, slightly crushed
- 3g (½ tsp) dried sage
- 3g (½ tsp) onion powder
- 3g (½ tsp) garlic powder
- 1g (⅛ tsp) cayenne pepper

### INSTRUCTIONS

1. In a bowl, mix the pork, salt, black pepper, thyme, fennel seeds, sage, onion powder, garlic powder, and cayenne pepper. Mix the ingredients until smooth and refrigerate for 2 hours. After, form the mixture into 4 patties.
2. Set the air fryer to 200°C (400°F) for 10 minutes.
3. Grease the air fryer basket cooking spray and lay in the patties without overlapping. Cook them for 5 minutes per side or until they are golden brown and cooked though.
4. Remove the sausage patties onto a plate and serve with other breakfast options or with your favourite morning sauce.

*Servings: 4*

## TOTAL CALORIES: 385
Protein: 18.38g | Fats: 25.1g | Carbs: 20.11g

## INGREDIENTS

For the breading:
- 110g (½ cup) breadcrumbs
- 8g (½ tbsp) maple sugar
- A pinch or two of smoked paprika

For the egg mixture:
- 1 large egg
- 5ml (1 tsp) Dijon mustard
- 15ml (1 tbsp) maple syrup
- 3 to 5ml (½ to 1 tsp) liquid smoke

For the eggs:
- 4 large hard- or soft-boiled eggs
- 225g (8 oz) sausage, removed from the casings
- Cooking spray
- Salad green for serving
- Sliced tomatoes for serving

For the sauce:
- 30ml (2 tbsp) soured cream
- 5g (1 tsp) maple sugar

## INSTRUCTIONS

For the breading:

1. On a plate, mix the breadcrumbs, maple sugar, and paprika.

For the egg mixture:

2. Crack the egg into a bowl and whisk in the mustard, maple syrup, and liquid smoke until smooth.

For the scotch eggs:

3. Peel the eggs.
4. Divide the sausage into four and tightly press each sausage portion onto each egg.
5. Dip the wrapped eggs in the egg mixture and roll well in the breading.
6. Set the air fryer to 190°C (375°F) for 10 minutes.
7. Mist the air fryer basket with cooking spray and place in the eggs.
8. Fry for 4 to 5 minutes per side or until they are golden brown.

For the sauce:

9. In a bowl, mix the soured cream and maple syrup until smooth.
10. When the scotch eggs are ready, transfer them to a plate.
11. Serve them with sauce and some salad greens and sliced tomatoes.

# PECAN DRIZZLE CINNAMON ROLLS

*Servings: 4*

## TOTAL CALORIES: 1734
Protein: 17.86g | Fats: 131.31g | Carbs: 136.7g

## INGREDIENTS

- Butter for greasing

For the dough:

- 225g (1 cup) all-purpose flour
- 5g (1 tsp) baking powder
- 1g (⅛ tsp) baking soda
- 20g (4 tsp) granulated sugar
- 1g (¼ tsp) salt
- 60g (4 tbsp) cold butter, cut into cubes
- 80ml (2/3 cup) whole milk

For the cinnamon filling:

- 30ml (2 tbsp) melted butter
- ½ cup brown sugar
- 1 tsp ground cinnamon

For the pecan drizzle:

- 110g (½ cup) unsalted butter
- 170g (¾ cup) dark brown sugar, packed
- 1g (¼ tsp) ground cinnamon
- 80ml (2/3 cup) double cream
- 10ml (2 tsp) vanilla extract
- 1g (¼ tsp) salt
- 110g (½ cup) pecans, roughly chopped
- 340g (1½ cups) pecans, halved

## INSTRUCTIONS

1. Preheat the air fryer to 160°C (320°F). Grease a round baking dish (that is a good fit for your air fryer) with butter and set aside.

For the dough:

2. In a bowl, mix the flour, baking powder, baking soda, sugar, and salt. Mix in the butter until turned into fine crumbs and then pour on the milk. Mix well until smooth batter forms.
3. Roll the dough on a floured surface into a 22 x 30cm rectangle.

For the cinnamon filling:

4. In a bowl, mix the butter, brown sugar, and ground cinnamon. Spread the mixture on the dough leaving about 2cm of one long end for sealing. Roll the dough from the opposite longer side over the filling towards the empty end. After, cut the dough into 6 to 8 pieces and fit them into the baking dish.
5. Place the dish in the air fryer, set the timer for 14 minutes, and bake for 10 to 14 minutes or until the cinnamon rolls rise and set.

For the pecan drizzle:

6. While the cinnamon rolls bake, in a bowl, mix the butter, brown sugar, and cinnamon. Whisk in the double cream, vanilla, and salt until smooth. Fold in the pecans (halved and chopped) until well-combined.
7. When the cinnamon rolls are ready, take them out and let them rest for 5 minutes. After, transfer them to a serving platter and spread on the pecan-butter drizzle.

# 5 | OH-SO-HEALTHY SNACKS

*Healthy snacks are a great way to fill up any day. Look around you and you can find an ingredient or two that can be transformed into hearty, nutritious snacks. In this collection, I create some sumptuous snacks from everyday ingredients available in my pantry that are also ready in little time.*

DON'T FORGET TO GET THE

**TOP RECIPES** FROM THIS BOOK
AS

**A FREE DOWNLOADABLE PDF IN COLOUR**

**SCAN THE QR CODE BELOW**

*Just follow the steps below to access it via the QR Code (the picture code at the bottom of this page) or click the link if you are reading this on your Phone / Device.*

1. Unlock your phone & open up the phone's camera
2. Make sure you are using the "back" camera (as if you were taking a photo of someone) and point it towards the QR code at the bottom of the page.
3. Tap your phone's screen exactly where the QR code is.
4. A link / pop up will appear. Simply tap that (and make sure you have internet connection) and the FREE PDF containing all of the colored images should appear.

# BANANA CRISPS

*Servings: 4*

**TOTAL CALORIES: 145**
Protein: 1.05g | Fats: 6.97g |
Carbs: 22.09g

## INGREDIENTS

- 4 fresh ripe and firm bananas, peeled
- 15ml (1 tbsp) fresh lemon juice
- 5ml (1 tsp) olive oil
- A pinch of salt

## INSTRUCTIONS

1. Use a mandoline to slice the bananas very thinly and place them in a bowl. Add the lemon juice, olive oil, and salt. Toss them well.
2. Set the air fryer to 180°C (360°F) for 12 minutes.
3. Add the banana to the air fryer basket in a single layer and bake for 12 minutes or until they are crispy. Meanwhile, shake the basket after 6 minutes of cooking.
4. Pour the banana chips into a bowl and let them cool completely. Enjoy them.
5. Preserve any extras in an airtight container or zipper bag on your countertop for up to a week.

# CARROT CHIPS

*Servings: 4*

**TOTAL CALORIES: 89**
Protein: 0.67g | Fats: 6.92g |
Carbs: 6.9g

## INGREDIENTS

- 4 large carrots
- 30ml (2 tbsp) olive oil
- 5g (1 tsp) sea salt

## INSTRUCTIONS

1. Using a mandoline, slice the carrots very thinly. Add them to a bowl and toss them with the olive oil and salt.
2. Set the air fryer to 180°C (360°F) for 12 minutes.
3. Add the carrots to the air fryer basket in a single layer and bake for 12 minutes or until they are crispy. Meanwhile, shake the basket after 6 minutes of cooking.
4. Pour the ready carrot chips into a bowl to cool completely. Serve after.
5. Preserve extras in an airtight container on your countertop for up to a week.

## CHEESE AND BASIL SAUSAGE ROLLS

*Servings: 4+*

**TOTAL CALORIES: 807**
Protein: 56.96g | Fats: 50.47g
| Carbs: 30.02g

### INGREDIENTS

- 450g (1 lb) beef mince
- 250g (½ lb) sausage beef mince
- 56g (¼ cup) tomato paste
- 75g (1/3 cup) chopped fresh basil
- 75g (1/3 cup) stuffed green olives, sliced
- 75g (1/3 cup) shredded mozzarella cheese
- 75g (1/3 cup) grated Parmesan cheese
- 4 sheets frozen puff pastry, defrosted
- 1 egg, beaten

### INSTRUCTIONS

1. Add the beef mince and sausage beef mince to a pot and cook on a stove-top over medium heat for 10 minutes or until brown. Season with salt and black pepper.
2. Take off the heat and stir in the tomato paste, basil, olives, and cheeses.
3. Lay the puff pastry sheets on a clean flat surface and spread the sausage mixture on top, leaving about 2cm space along their longer edges for sealing. Roll the pastry over the filling and seal at the end.
4. Cut each pastry into 6 pieces, brush with the egg, and lay them in the air fryer basket in a single layer.
5. Set the air fryer to 200°C (400°F) for 12 minutes and bake for 10 to 12 minutes or until they are golden brown.
6. Transfer them to a wire rack to cool and serve.

## CHEESY BEANS ON TOAST

*Servings: 4*

**TOTAL CALORIES: 311**
Protein: 14.72g | Fats: 18.14g
| Carbs: 22.25g

### INGREDIENTS

- 4 bread slices
- 15ml (1 tbsp) butter
- 225g (1 cup) baked beans
- 5ml (1 tsp) Worcestershire sauce
- 170g (6 oz) white cheddar cheese, sliced

### INSTRUCTIONS

1. Spread the butter on both sides of the bread.
2. In a ramekin, mix the baked beans with Worcestershire sauce.
3. Set the air fryer to 180°C (360°F) for 6 minutes.
4. Place the bread in the air fryer and set the baked beans by them. Toast the bread for 2 to 3 minutes per side while the baked beans warm alongside.
5. Take out the bread and spread the baked beans on them. Lay the cheese on them.
6. Carefully lay the loaded toasts in the air fryer and bake for 1 to 2 minutes or until the cheese melts.
7. Take out the toasts and serve them warm.

## CHEESE RAVIOLI AND BASIL TOMATO SAUCE

*Servings: 4*

**TOTAL CALORIES: 507**
Protein: 21.49g | Fats: 11.68g | Carbs: 78.14g

### INGREDIENTS

- 225g (1 cup) breadcrumbs
- 15g (1 tbsp) dried mixed herbs
- 60g (¼ cup) shredded Parmesan cheese plus extra for garnish
- 110g (½ cup) all-purpose flour / gluten-free flour
- 2 large eggs, lightly beaten
- 1 package (9 oz) frozen cheese ravioli, thawed
- Cooking spray
- 240ml (1 cup) tomato sauce, warmed
- 15g (1 tbsp) chopped fresh basil plus extra for garnish

### INSTRUCTIONS

1. On a plate, mix the breadcrumbs, mixed herbs, and Parmesan cheese. Put the flour and eggs in separate bowls.
2. Set the air fryer to 175°C (350°F) for 10 minutes.
3. Dredge the ravioli in the flour, then dip in the eggs, and coat well in the breadcrumb mixture.
4. Mist the air fryer basket with cooking spray and add the ravioli in a single layer. Fry for 5 minutes per side or until they are golden brown.
5. Remove them onto a plate when ready and garnish with some Parmesan cheese and basil.
6. In a bowl, mix the tomato sauce with basil and serve with the ravioli.

## CHOCOLATE PISTACHIO FUDGE BROWNIES

*Servings: 4*

**TOTAL CALORIES: 2081**
Protein: 39.42g | Fats: 112.61g | Carbs: 257.19g

### INGREDIENTS

- 225g (1 cup) butter plus extra for greasing the tin
- 280g (1¼ cups) dark chocolate chips
- 170g (¾ cup) unsweetened cocoa powder
- 450g (2 cups) white sugar
- 60g (¼ cup) brown sugar
- 15ml (1 tbsp) vanilla extract
- 3g (½ tsp) salt
- 4 large eggs
- 280g (1¼ cups) all-purpose flour / gluten-free flour
- 225g (1 cup) chopped pistachios
- 110g (½ cup) dried cranberries, chopped

### INSTRUCTIONS

1. Grease a rectangular tin (one that can fit into your air fryer) with butter and put it aside.
2. Put the butter in a safe microwave bowl and melt for a few seconds. Add the chocolate chips and stir until they are melted.
3. Mix in the cocoa powder, white and brown sugar, vanilla, and salt until smooth. Crack in the eggs and whisk until smooth. Add the flour and mix until smooth batter forms. Fold in the pistachios and cranberries.
4. Pour the batter into the tin and smooth it out with a spoon or butter knife.
5. Set the air fryer to 160°C (320°F) for 25 minutes.
6. Place the tin in the air fryer and bake for 20 to 25 minutes or until the brownie sets when tested with a toothpick.
7. Take out the pan and leave the brownie to cool in the pan.
8. After, turn it over onto a wire rack and cut into brownie sizes. Serve.

## CINNAMON APPLE CRISPS

*Servings: 4*

**TOTAL CALORIES: 149**
Protein: 0.63g | Fats: 3.77g |
Carbs: 31.84g

### INGREDIENTS

- 4 large apples
- 30 (2 tsp) cinnamon
- 15ml (1 tbsp) olive or avocado oil

### INSTRUCTIONS

1. Using a mandolin, slice the apples very thinly and add them to a bowl. Add the cinnamon and oil and toss until well coated.
2. Set the air fryer to 150°C (300°F) for 25 minutes.
3. Pour the apples in the air fryer basket and bake for 20 to 25 minutes or until they are golden brown and crispy.
4. Transfer them to a bowl or cooling surface and let them cool completely.
5. Enjoy them and preserve extras in an airtight container on your countertop for up to a week.

## CREAM AND JAM SCONES

*Servings: 4*

**TOTAL CALORIES: 490**
Protein: 6.69g | Fats: 32.01g |
Carbs: 44.33g

### INGREDIENTS

- 175g (¾ cup) all-purpose flour
- 3g (½ tsp) baking powder
- 45g (1/6 cup) butter, cold and cut into small cubes
- 30g (2 tbsp) caster sugar
- 85ml (5½ tbsp) warm milk
- ½ lemon, juiced
- 3ml (½ tsp) vanilla extract
- 240ml (1 cup) double cream
- 60g (¼ cup) icing sugar

### INSTRUCTIONS

1. Set the air fryer to 200°C (400°F) for 8 minutes.
2. Combine the flour and baking powder in a bowl. Mix in the butter until finely crumbly and mix in the sugar. Add the milk, vanilla, and lemon juice. Mix until a sticky dough forms.
3. Dust a surface with flour, place the dough on top, and knead until the dough for a few minutes or until covered with flour. Spread the dough out into a 3 cm thick disc and cut out 4 scones using a 5cm fluted cookie cutter. Brush the dough pieces with milk.
4. Line the air fryer basket with parchment paper and place the dough on top with 3cm intervals between them.
5. Bake for 7 to 8 minutes or until golden brown and well-risen.
6. Remove the scones onto a wire rack to cool completely.
7. Meanwhile, in a bowl, whisk the double cream and icing sugar until thickened.
8. Slice the scones in halves, spread the jam on the bottom parts, top with the cream and cover with the tops of the scones.

## CURRY BREADED AVOCADO FRIES

*Servings: 4*

**TOTAL CALORIES: 807**
Protein: 21.97g | Fats: 55.85g | Carbs: 58.53

### INGREDIENTS

- 3 slightly under-ripe avocados
- 225g (1 cup) panko breadcrumbs
- 110g (½ cup) grated Parmesan cheese
- 3g (½ tsp) curry powder
- 3g (½ tsp) black pepper
- 2 large eggs, beaten
- Cooking spray

For the dipping sauce:
- 120ml (½ cup) salad cream
- 30ml (2 tbsp) hot sauce or to taste

### INSTRUCTIONS

1. Pit and peel the avocados and slice each half into 4 to 5 pieces.
2. Mix the breadcrumbs, Parmesan cheese, curry powder, and black pepper on a plate. Pour the eggs on a separate plate.
3. Dip the avocados in the eggs and coat well with the breadcrumb mixture.
4. Set the air fryer to 175°C (350°F) for 6 minutes.
5. Grease the air fryer with cooking spray and place the breaded avocados in a single layer. Bake for 3 minutes per side or until they are golden brown.

Meanwhile, make the spicy salad cream:
6. In a bowl, mix the salad cream and hot sauce until even in colour.
7. Serve the avocado fries when they are ready with the spicy salad cream.

## DRIED MANGOES

*Servings: 4*

**TOTAL CALORIES: 101**
Protein: 1.38g | Fats: 0.64g | Carbs: 25.17g

### INGREDIENTS

- 2 large mangoes

### INSTRUCTIONS

1. Peel the mangoes and slice them thinly.
2. Set the air fryer to 80°C (160°F) for 5 hours.
3. Lay the mangoes in the air fryer basket and dehydrate them for 4 to 5 hours.
4. Remove the dried mangoes into a bowl to cool completely.
5. Enjoy and preserve any extras in an airtight container or zipper bag at room temperature for up to 2 weeks.

## FLAPJACKS WITH FRUITS AND NUTS

*Servings: 4*

**TOTAL CALORIES: 1222**
Protein: 26.59g | Fats: 82.01g | Carbs: 105.87g

### INGREDIENTS

- 225g melted butter, plus extra greasing the tin
- 60ml (4 tbsp) honey
- 75g (3 tbsp) caster sugar
- 350g (1½ cups) porridge oats
- 225g (1 cup) dried fruits and nuts mix

### INSTRUCTIONS

1. Grease a rectangle baking tin (with size that can fit into your air fryer) with butter. Put it aside.
2. In a bowl, mix the butter, honey, and sugar until smooth. Stir in the oats and dried fruits and nuts mix until well-distributed.
3. Add the mixture to the baking tin and spread out with your spoon until even and well tucked into the corners and sides.
4. Set the air fryer to 180°C (360°F) for 10 to 15 minutes.
5. Place the tin in the air fryer and bake for 10 to 15 minutes or until the flapjacks are golden and compact.
6. Take out the tin and let it cool completely in the pan.
7. After, turn the flapjacks over onto a chopping board and cut into 16 bars.

## FRUIT WINDERS

*Servings: 4*

**TOTAL CALORIES: 159**
Protein: 2.38g | Fats: 0.47g | Carbs: 40.63g

### INGREDIENTS

- 450g (1 lb) fresh strawberries, hulled, rinsed, and sliced
- 1 mandarin orange, juiced
- 1 (820g / 30 oz) can peaches in juice, drained
- 15ml (1 tbsp) agave syrup

### INSTRUCTIONS

1. In a blender, add the strawberries, half of the orange juice, and agave syrup. Blend the strawberries until smooth. Pour the strawberry puree into a bowl and rinse the blender.
2. Add the peaches and remaining orange juice into the blender and blend until smooth.
3. Into some fruit leather trays (with good size for your air fryer), pour the strawberry and peach purees separately, and smooth them out.
4. Set the air fryer to 60°C (120°F) for 15 hours.
5. Place the fruit trays in the air fryer and dehydrate the fruit purees for 12 to 15 hours or until the fruit winders are no longer tacky.
6. Take out the trays and let them cool completely.
7. Roll each fruit winder and place them in containers. Refrigerate them and enjoy them for up to 2 weeks.

# GARLIC KALE CHIPS

*Servings: 4*

**TOTAL CALORIES: 219**
Protein: 16.69g | Fats: 6.89g | Carbs: 6.89g

## INGREDIENTS

- 1.5kg (6 cups) kale leaves, torn
- 15ml (1 tbsp) olive or avocado oil
- 10g (2 tsp) nutritional yeast
- 1g (¼ tsp) garlic powder
- Salt and black pepper to taste

## INSTRUCTIONS

1. Rinse the kale well and pat them completely dry with paper towels.
2. Add them to a bowl and season with the oil, nutritional yeast, garlic powder, salt, and black pepper. Toss to coat evenly.
3. Set the air fryer to 150°C (300°F) for 5 minutes.
4. Working in batches, add about a cup of the kale to the air fryer basket and bake for 7 to 10 minutes or until they are crispy. Meanwhile, shake the basket or stir through them after 4 to 5 minutes of cooking.
5. Pour them into a bowl and bake the rest.

# GINGER NUT SNAPS

*Servings: 4*

**TOTAL CALORIES: 977**
Protein: 16.47g | Fats: 44.75g | Carbs: 128.16g

## INGREDIENTS

- 450g (2 cups) all-purpose flour / gluten-free flour
- 110g (½ cup) ground almonds (optional for nut-free version)
- 10g (2 tsp) baking soda
- 5g (1 tsp) ground cinnamon
- 3g (½ tsp) ground cardamom
- 10g (2 tsp) ground ginger
- 5g (1 tsp) ground cloves
- 5g (1 tsp) salt
- 170g (¾ cup) unsalted butter, room temperature
- 60ml (¼ cup) dark molasses
- 180ml (¾ cup) brown sugar
- 1 large egg, cracked into a bowl
- 10ml (2 tsp) vanilla extract

## INSTRUCTIONS

1. In one bowl, mix the flour, ground almonds, baking soda, cinnamon, cardamom, ginger, cloves, and salt.
2. In another bowl, whisk the butter, molasses, brown sugar, egg, and vanilla. Combine the flour and egg mixtures and whisk until smooth, thick dough forms.
3. Set the air fryer to 160°C (320°F) for 7 minutes.
4. Line the air fryer basket with parchment paper.
5. Using a cookie scoop, add 1½ tbsp portions of the dough onto the parchment paper with 3cm intervals between each.
6. Bake for 5 to 7 minutes or until the cookies are golden brown and set.
7. Transfer the biscuits to a wire rack to cool and enjoy them.

# HONEY CINNA- MON CHICKPEAS

*Servings: 4*

## TOTAL CALORIES: 552
Protein: 4.03g | Fats: 52.57g | Carbs: 21.93g

## INGREDIENTS

- 225g (8 oz) canned chickpeas, rinsed and drained
- 30ml (2 tbsp) honey
- 15ml (1 tbsp) coconut oil
- 3g (½ tsp) ground cinnamon
- A pinch of salt

## INSTRUCTIONS

1. Pat dry the chickpeas and add them to a bowl. Add the honey, coconut oil, cinnamon, and salt to a bowl, and toss well.
2. Set the air fryer to 190°C (375°F) for 15 minutes.
3. Line the air fryer basket with parchment paper and spread the chickpeas on top.
4. Roast for 12 to 15 minutes or until they are golden brown and crunchy.

# PORK PIES

*Servings: 4*

## TOTAL CALORIES: 1677
Protein: 48.86g | Fats:108.63g | Carbs: 123.84g

## INGREDIENTS

- 15g (1 tbsp) corn starch
- 420ml (1¼ cups) reduced-sodium chicken broth
- 900g (2 lb) pork mince
- 3 garlic cloves, minced
- Salt and black pepper to taste
- 1g (¼ tsp) ground nutmeg
- 1g (¼ tsp) ground cloves
- 1g (¼ tsp) cayenne pepper
- 4 sheets refrigerated pie crust
- 1 large egg
- 10ml (2 tsp) milk

## INSTRUCTIONS

1. In a pot, mix the corn starch and chicken broth until smooth. Cook on a stovetop over medium heat for 1 to 2 minutes or until thickened. Take off the heat.
2. Add the pork to a pot and cook over medium heat for 10 minutes. Season with the garlic, salt, and black pepper. Cook for 1 minute and season with the nutmeg, cloves, and cayenne pepper. Stir in the thickened broth, simmer for 1 to 2 minutes, and turn the heat off.
3. Spoon the mixture into 8 to 12 muffin cups and set them aside.
4. Roll out the pie crusts and cut out 8 to 12 (10cm) circles. Place each circle on each muffin cup and crimp the edges to seal. After, create 1 or 2 dents in the centre of each crust to release steam when cooking.
5. Crack the egg into a bowl and whisk with the milk. Brush the egg wash on each crust.
6. Set the air fryer to 200°C (400°F) for 20 minutes.
7. Place the pies in the air fryer and bake for 15 to 20 minutes or until golden brown on top and the filling warmed through.
8. Take out the pies and let them cool slightly before serving.

## ROASTED CORN ON THE COB WITH GARLIC-CHIVE BUTTER

*Servings: 4*

**TOTAL CALORIES: 218**
Protein: 3.73g | Fats: 15.86g | Carbs: 19.57g

### INGREDIENTS

- 4 ears fresh yellow corn, husk and silk removed
- 10ml (2 tsp) olive oil
- 3g (½ tsp) kosher salt
- 60g (¼ cup) salted butter, softened
- 1g (¼ tsp) black pepper
- 30g (2 tbsp) finely chopped fresh chives
- Extra chopped chives for garnish

### INSTRUCTIONS

1. Rub the corn with olive oil and season with salt.
2. Set the air fryer to 200°C (400°F) for 14 minutes.
3. Place the corn in the air fryer and roast for 12 to 14 minutes or until they are golden brown and tender. Turn the corn every 2 to 3 minutes to ensure it cooks evenly on every side.
4. While the corn cooks, in a bowl, mix the butter, black pepper, and chives.
5. Spread the butter on the corn when ready. Garnish with chives and serve them.

## SALTED BEET CHIPS

*Servings: 4*

**TOTAL CALORIES: 65**
Protein: 1.32g | Fats: 3.51g | Carbs: 7.84g

### INGREDIENTS

- 4 beetroots, peeled
- 15ml (1 tbsp) olive oil
- Salt to taste plus extra for topping

### INSTRUCTIONS

1. Using a mandoline, slice the beets very thinly. Add them to a bowl and toss them with the olive oil and salt.
2. Set the air fryer to 180°C (360°F) for 12 minutes.
3. Add the beets to the air fryer basket without overlapping and bake for 12 minutes or until they are crispy. Meanwhile, shake the basket after 6 minutes of cooking.
4. Pour the ready beet chips into a bowl to cool completely. Sprinkle with some salt and serve.
5. Preserve extras in an airtight container on your countertop for up to a week.

## SPICY CAULIFLOWER FLORETS

*Servings: 4*

### TOTAL CALORIES: 281
Protein: 11.81g | Fats: 4.89g | Carbs: 48.81g

### INGREDIENTS

- 225g (1 cup) breadcrumbs
- 8g (1½ tsp) smoked paprika
- 3g (½ tsp) onion powder
- 3g (½ tsp) garlic powder
- 3g (½ tsp) cayenne pepper
- 1g (¼ heaping tsp) sea salt
- 1 large egg
- 450g (2 cups) small cauliflower florets
- Cooking spray
- Lemon wedges, for serving

### INSTRUCTIONS

1. In a bowl, mix the breadcrumbs, paprika, onion powder, garlic powder, cayenne pepper, and salt. Crack the egg into another bowl and beat.
2. Dip the cauliflower florets in the egg and coat well in the breadcrumb mixture. You can coat the cauliflower a second time for extra crunch.
3. Set the air fryer to 185°C (370°F) for 12 minutes.
4. Grease the air fryer basket with cooking spray and add the breaded cauliflower in a single layer.
5. Fry for 5 to 6 minutes per side or until golden brown.
6. Take them out onto a plate and fry any extras.
7. Serve them with your favourite dipping sauce.

## VIENNESE WHIRLS

*Servings: 4*

### TOTAL CALORIES: 994
Protein: 6.03g | Fats: 61.43g | Carbs: 106.07g

### INGREDIENTS

For the cakes:
- 200g (¾ cup) slightly salted butter, softened
- 50g (1/6 cup) icing sugar
- 10ml (2 tsp) vanilla extract
- 200g (1 cup) all-purpose flour / gluten-free flour
- 10g (2 tsp) cornflour
- 3g (½ tsp) baking powder

For the filling:
- 100g (½ cup) butter, softened
- 170g (¾ cup) icing sugar
- 5ml (1 tsp) vanilla extract
- 60g (¼ cup) raspberry jam or strawberry jam

### INSTRUCTIONS

For the cakes:
1. Set the air fryer to 180°C (360°F) for 12 minutes.
2. Add the butter and icing sugar to a bowl and whisk with an electric hand mixer until pale and fluffy. Add the vanilla and beat until well-incorporated. Sift in the flour, cornflour, and baking powder and mix until smooth and tacky batter forms. Spoon the batter into a piping bag with a large star nozzle.
3. Line the air fryer basket with parchment paper and pipe 5cm diameter swirly circles on the paper with 3cm intervals between each.
4. Bake in the air fryer for 10 to 12 minutes or until they are golden brown and set.
5. Transfer them to a wire rack to completely cool and make more with the remaining batter.

For the filling:
6. Beat the butter and icing sugar in a bowl with an electric hand mixer until smooth. Add the vanilla and incorporate well.
7. Spread the jam on half of each cake (the flat sides) and top with the vanilla icing. Cover with the other cakes (with the flat side facing inwards).

# 6 | SUCH FILLING SIDES

*In my opinion, the perfect side dish achieves three things. It hits with a salivating flavour from afar, comfortably satisfies, and is versatile to pair with as many dishes as possible. These side dishes are great for everyday servings, they are budget-friendly, and seamless to make.*

## DON'T FORGET TO GET THE
## **TOP RECIPES** FROM THIS BOOK
## AS
## **A FREE DOWNLOADABLE PDF IN COLOUR**

**SCAN THE QR CODE BELOW**

*Just follow the steps below to access it via the QR Code (the picture code at the bottom of this page) or click the link if you are reading this on your Phone / Device.*

1. Unlock your phone & open up the phone's camera
2. Make sure you are using the "back" camera (as if you were taking a photo of someone) and point it towards the QR code at the bottom of the page.
3. Tap your phone's screen exactly where the QR code is.
4. A link / pop up will appear. Simply tap that (and make sure you have internet connection) and the FREE PDF containing all of the colored images should appear.

## BACON-STUFFED MUSHROOMS

*Servings: 4*

### TOTAL CALORIES: 234
Protein: 12.78g | Fats: 16.41g | Carbs: 9.03g

### INGREDIENTS

- 8 white button mushrooms
- 110g (4 oz) soft cheese
- 30g (2 tbsp) breadcrumbs
- 1g (¼ tsp) ground sage
- 60g (¼ cup) chopped cooked bacon
- 60g (¼ cup) grated Old Winchester cheese

### INSTRUCTIONS

1. De-stem the mushrooms and rinse them well. After, pat them dry with paper towels.
2. Mix the soft cheese, breadcrumbs, sage, bacon, and Old Winchester cheese.
3. Set the air fryer to 175°C (350°F) for 8 minutes.
4. Set the mushrooms in the air fryer basket and bake for 6 to 8 minutes or until they are golden brown and tender.
5. Remove the mushrooms to a serving plate and serve warm.

## BREADED CAULIFLOWER

*Servings: 4*

### TOTAL CALORIES: 281
Protein: 11.81g | Fats: 4.89g | Carbs: 48.81g

### INGREDIENTS

- 225g (1 cup) panko bread crumbs
- 3g (½ tsp) onion powder
- 3g (½ tsp) garlic powder
- 8g (1½ tsp) smoked paprika
- 3g (½ tsp) cayenne
- 1g (¼ tsp) salt or to taste
- 1 large egg
- 450g (2 cups) small cauliflower florets
- Cooking spray

### INSTRUCTIONS

1. On a plate, mix the breadcrumbs, onion powder, garlic powder, paprika, cayenne pepper, and salt. Also, crack the egg into a bowl and beat it.
2. Dip each cauliflower floret in the egg and coat well with the breadcrumbs. You can repeat the breading process a second time for extra crunch.
3. Set the air fryer to 185°C (370°F) for 12 minutes.
4. Mist the air fryer basket with cooking spray and add the cauliflower in a single layer.
5. Fry for 4 to 6 minutes per side or until they are golden brown and the cauliflower is tender.
6. Transfer them to a plate and serve warm with soup.

## BROCCOLI WITH OLD WINCHESTER

*Servings: 4*

**TOTAL CALORIES:1022**
Protein: 4.68g | Fats: 112.23g | Carbs: 2.87g

### INGREDIENTS

• 1 head of broccoli, chopped into florets
• 2 garlic cloves, minced
• 30ml (2 tbsp) extra virgin olive oil
• Salt and black pepper to taste
• 60g (¼ cup) grated Old Winchester cheese

### INSTRUCTIONS

1. Toss the broccoli with the garlic, olive oil, salt, black pepper, and cheese.
2. Set the air fryer to 180°C (360°F) for 5 minutes.
3. Add the broccoli to the air fryer basket and bake for 4 to 5 minutes or until it is tender.
4. Plate the broccoli and serve warm.

## BUTTERED PARSNIP CHIPS

*Servings: 4*

**TOTAL CALORIES:173**
Protein: 2.09g | Fats: 9.01g | Carbs: 23.03g

### INGREDIENTS

• 450g (1 lb) parsnips
• 10 to 15ml (2 to 3 tsp) melted butter
• 15g (1 tbsp) garlic granules
• Salt to taste
• Chopped fresh parsley for garnish

### INSTRUCTIONS

1. Scrub the parsnips thoroughly, cut off their heads and bottoms, and cut them into chips shapes.
2. Add them to a bowl with the butter, garlic, and salt. Toss well.
3. Set the air fryer to 180°C (360°F) for 14 minutes.
4. Add the parsnips to the air fryer basket and fry for 14 minutes or until they are golden brown and tender while shaking the basket 2 to 3 times during cooking.
5. Plate the parsnips, garnish them with parsley, and serve warm.

## CAULIFLOWER CHEESE WITH TUNA

*Servings: 4*

**TOTAL CALORIES: 361**
Protein: 15.9g | Fats: 23.67g |
Carbs: 23.19g

### INGREDIENTS

- 1 cauliflower
- 40g (3 tbsp) butter
- 50g (3 tbsp) plain flour
- 5g (1 tsp)
- 475ml (2 cups) milk
- 130g (5 oz) grated mature cheddar cheese
- 5ml (1 tsp) English mustard
- 110g (3.8 oz) can tuna in water, drained

### INSTRUCTIONS

1. Cook the cauliflower in salted boiling water until they are tender with a bite. Drain them well and set them aside.
2. Melt the butter in a pot and whisk in the flour until it is light golden. Add the milk and whisk until smooth. Add the mustard and one-third of the cheddar cheese, and whisk until the cheese melts.
3. Set the air fryer to 190°C (380°F) for 20 minutes.
4. Spread the cauliflower and tuna in a baking dish (that can fit into your air fryer) and drizzle the cheese sauce all over them. Scatter the remaining cheese on top.
5. Bake for 18 to 20 mins or until the cheese melts and it is golden brown.
6. Take out the dish and serve the cauliflower cheese warm.

## CHILLI CHEESE TOASTIES

*Servings: 4*

**TOTAL CALORIES: 252**
Protein: 14.74g | Fats: 15.4g |
Carbs: 13.29g

### INGREDIENTS

- 15g (1 tbsp) unsalted butter, at room temperature
- 4 bread slices
- 225g (1 cup) grated mozzarella cheese
- 110g (½ cup) chopped red sweet peppers
- 2 garlic cloves, minced
- 8g (½ tbsp) red chilli flakes
- 30g (2 tbsp) chopped fresh coriander

### INSTRUCTIONS

1. Spread the butter on both sides of each bread slice.
2. On one side of each, spread the mozzarella cheese, red sweet peppers, garlic, red chilli flakes, and coriander.
3. Set the air fryer to 175°C (350°F) for 5 minutes.
4. Place the loaded bread in the air fryer basket and toast for 3 to 5 minutes or until the cheese melts and the bread is golden brown.
5. Put the toasties on a plate and serve immediately.

## GARLIC CHEESE ASPARAGUS

*Servings: 4*

**TOTAL CALORIES: 255**
Protein: 15.15g | Fats: 16.09g |
Carbs: 6.51g

### INGREDIENTS

• 450g (1 lb) asparagus, hard stems removed
• 15ml (1 tbsp) olive oil
• 5g (1 tsp) garlic powder
• Salt and black pepper to taste
• 225g (1 cup) shredded mozzarella cheese

### INSTRUCTIONS

1. Line the air fryer basket with foil.
2. Add the asparagus to a bowl along with the olive oil, garlic powder, salt, and black pepper. Toss well and arrange them in the air fryer basket.
3. Set the air fryer to 200°C (400°F) for 8 minutes.
4. Cook the asparagus for 5 to 6 minutes or until they are tender.
5. Open the air fryer and sprinkle the mozzarella cheese on top. Bake further for 2 minutes or until the cheese melts.
6. Plate the cheesy asparagus and serve them warm.

## GARLIC COURGETTE

*Servings: 4*

**TOTAL CALORIES: 33**
Protein: 0.23g | Fats: 3.4g |
Carbs: 0.53g

### INGREDIENTS

• 2 courgettes
• 15ml (1 tbsp) olive oil
• 10g (2 tsp) garlic powder
• Salt and black pepper to taste

### INSTRUCTIONS

1. Cut the courgettes into 1.5cm slices and put them in a bowl. Toss them with the olive oil, garlic powder, salt, and black pepper.
2. Set the air fryer to 175°C (350°F) for 10 minutes.
3. Lay the courgette in the air fryer without overlapping and cook for them 5 minutes per side. When they are golden brown and tender, they are ready.
4. Put them on a plate and serve them warm.

# GREEN ONION CAKES

*Servings: 4*

## TOTAL CALORIES: 433
Protein: 8.4g | Fats: 16.08g | Carbs: 63.03g

## INGREDIENTS

For the dough:
- 2 cups all-purpose flour
- 3g (½ tsp) sea salt
- 10g (2 tsp) granulated sugar
- 110g (½ cup) hot water
- 60g (¼ cup) cool water

For the filling:
- 60g (¼ cup) all-purpose flour
- 75g (1/3 cup) unsalted butter, melted
- 3g (½ tsp) sea salt
- 8 green onions, finely chopped
- Cooking spray

## INSTRUCTIONS

For the dough:
1. In a large bowl, mix the flour, salt, and sugar. Slowly mix in the hot water with a fork and then mix in the cold water until a shaggy dough forms. Dust a working surface with flour and knead the dough for 3 minutes. Cover the dough and let it rest for 30 minutes.

For the filling:
2. While the dough rests, prepare the filling. In a bowl, mix the flour, butter, and salt.

Back to the dough:
3. Divide the dough into 6 balls.
4. Working with one dough ball at a time (keep the others covered), roll the dough on a floured surface into a rectangle. Then, sprinkle the filling mixture on top and spread a sixth of the green onions on top.
5. With the long side in front of you, roll the dough over the filling into a long thin log. Press the seams on the sides to seal and roll the log into a spiral shape. Tuck the edges underneath and cover. Repeat the other dough balls the same way.
6. When ready to bake, set the air fryer to 175°C (350°F) for 8 minutes.
7. Working with one dough ball at a time, uncover the dough ball and flatten it with your palms into a 20cm circle.
8. Mist the air fryer basket with cooking spray and place the dough in it. Bake for 5 minutes per side or until it is golden brown and cooked within.
9. Transfer it to a plate and bake the remaining 5 dough balls.
10. Slice them into triangles and serve them warm.

## HERB BUTTER POTATOES

*Servings: 4*

**TOTAL CALORIES: 112**
Protein: 2.87g | Fats: 2.28g | Carbs: 20.92g

### INGREDIENTS

- 450g (1 lb) potatoes
- 10 to 15g (2 to 3 tsp) melted butter
- 15g (1 tbsp) garlic granules
- 15g (1 tbsp) each chopped fresh parsley, thyme, and chives
- Salt to taste
- Chopped fresh parsley for garnish

### INSTRUCTIONS

1. Peel the potatoes and cut them into 3cm chunks.
2. Add them to a bowl and top with the butter, garlic, herbs, and salt. Toss them well.
3. Set the air fryer to 200°C (400°F) for 15 minutes.
4. Add the potatoes to the air fryer basket and bake for 10 to 15 minutes or until potatoes are golden brown and tender. Meanwhile, shake the basket 2 to 3 times through cooking.
5. Transfer the potatoes to a serving bowl, garnish with parsley and serve warm.

## LANCASHIRE BRUSSELS SPROUTS

*Servings: 4*

**TOTAL CALORIES: 137**
Protein: 7.6g | Fats: 8.26g | Carbs: 10.72g

### INGREDIENTS

- 450g (1 lb) Brussels sprouts
- 15ml (1 tbsp) olive oil
- 3g (½ tsp) garlic powder
- Salt and black pepper to taste
- 60g (¼ cup) grated Lancashire cheese

### INSTRUCTIONS

1. Trim the ends of the Brussels sprouts, remove their outer leaves, and cut them halves lengthwise. Place them in a bowl and add the olive oil, garlic powder, salt, and black pepper. Toss them well.
2. Set the air fryer to 200°C (400°F) for 6 minutes.
3. Add the Brussels sprouts in the air fryer basket and bake for 5 to 6 minutes or until they are tender, shaking the basket halfway through cooking.
4. Transfer them to a bowl and immediately toss them with the cheese.
5. Let the cheese melt over the Brussels sprouts and serve them warm.

# LOADED BAKED POTATOES

*Servings: 4*

## TOTAL CALORIES: 617
Protein: 16.08g | Fats: 33.79g | Carbs: 63.24g

## INGREDIENTS

- 4 large baking potatoes
- 30ml (2 tbsp) olive oil
- Salt and black pepper to taste

For the fillings and toppings (of your desired quantities):
- Butter
- Soured cream
- Shredded cheddar cheese
- Cooked crumbled bacon
- Sliced salad onions

## INSTRUCTIONS

1. Scrub the potatoes well and use a fork to prick holes all around them. Rub them with the olive oil, salt, and black pepper. Place them in the air fryer basket.
2. Set the air fryer to 200°C (400°F) for 40 minutes.
3. Cook the potatoes for 20 minutes, turn them and cook them again for 20 minutes or until they are tender.
4. Place the potatoes on a chopping board and let them cool to touch. Slice them in halves (all the way through, or not, is optional).
5. Gently squeeze out the flesh to the top without destroying the skins.
6. Fill them with some butter, soured cream, cheese, bacon, and green onions.
7. Serve the potatoes warm.

# POTATO GRATIN

*Servings: 4*

## TOTAL CALORIES: 730
Protein: 18.44g | Fats: 63.16g | Carbs: 24.63g

## INGREDIENTS

- 450g (1 lb) potatoes
- 480ml (2 cups) double cream
- 5g (1 tsp) garlic powder
- Salt and black pepper to taste
- 225 to 450g (1 to 2 cups) grated cheddar cheese

## INSTRUCTIONS

1. Peel and wash the potatoes. After, thinly slice and boil them in slightly salted water for 5 minutes or until they are starting to get tender.
2. Mix the double cream with the garlic powder, salt, and black pepper.
3. Set the air fryer to 175°C (350°F) for 30 minutes.
4. In a baking dish that can fit into your air fryer, lay out a third of the potatoes, top with a third of the cooking cream, and then a third of the cheddar cheese. Repeat the layering process two more times.
5. Place the dish in the air fryer and bake for 30 minutes or until the cheese is melted and golden brown, sauce bubbly, and potatoes tender.
6. Take out the dish and let cool for 5 to 10 minutes before serving.

## RUMBLEDETHUMPS

*Servings: 4*

**TOTAL CALORIES: 291**
Protein: 6.08g | Fats: 17.59g |
Carbs: 29.99g

### INGREDIENTS

• 450g (1 lb) large potatoes, peeled and cut into large chunks
• 400g (14 oz) swede, peeled and cut into large chunks
• 75g (2¾ oz) butter
• 250g (9 oz) savoy cabbage, finely sliced
• Salt and black pepper to taste
• 25g (1 oz) cheddar cheese, grated

### INSTRUCTIONS

1. Cook the potatoes and turnips in a pot of salted boiling water until they are tender. Drain them well and return them to the pot.
2. Melt half of the butter in a frying pan, then sauté the cabbage for 5 minutes or until tender and retains its colour.
3. Add the cabbage to the potatoes and turnips, then the remaining butter, salt, and black pepper. Mash everything until mostly smooth.
4. Spread the mashed food into a baking dish (one that can fit into your air fryer) and spread the cheddar cheese on top.
5. Set the air fryer to 175°C (350°F) for 30 minutes.
6. Place the dish in the air fryer and bake for 25 to 30 minutes or until the cheese melts and is golden brown.
7. Take out the dish and serve your rumbledethumps warm.

## STUFFED TOMATOES

*Servings: 4*

**TOTAL CALORIES: 669**
Protein: 32.63g | Fats: 41.05g |
Carbs: 42.59g

### INGREDIENTS

• 4 large tomatoes
• 15ml (1 tbsp) olive oil
• ¼ yellow onion, finely chopped
• 5g (1 tsp) minced garlic
• 225g (½ lb) sweet sausage, casings removed
• Salt and black pepper to taste
• 60g (¼ cup) chopped fresh basil
• 170g (¾ cup) breadcrumbs
• 60g (¼ cup) grated Parmesan cheese
• 225g (1 cup) grated mozzarella cheese

### INSTRUCTIONS

1. Slice the heads off the tomatoes and core them to make enough room for the filling. Chop the filling and add them to a bowl. Then, turn the tomatoes upside down onto a paper towel to drain off some liquid.
2. Heat the olive oil in a skillet over medium heat. Add the onion and sauté for 3 minutes or until tender. Stir in the garlic, cook for 1 minute, and break the sausage in. Stir and cook for 5 to 8 minutes to develop its flavour. Turn the heat off and stir in the basil, breadcrumbs, Parmesan, and mozzarella.
3. Spoon the breadcrumbs mixture into the tomatoes to the brim of it and a bit over.
4. Set the air fryer to 175°C (350°F) for 10 minutes.
5. Set the tomatoes in the air fryer basket and bake for 8 to 10 minutes or until the tomatoes are tender.
6. Take them out when ready and serve warm.

## SWEET PEA CASSEROLE

*Servings: 4*

**TOTAL CALORIES: 868**
Protein: 27.43g | Fats: 58.38g | Carbs: 59.9g

### INGREDIENTS

- 1 (300g / 10.75 oz) can condensed cream of mushroom soup
- 5g (1 tsp) garlic powder
- 240ml (1 cup) soured cream
- 225g (1 cup) grated cheddar cheese, divided
- 110g (½ cup) butter, melted
- 2 (410g / 14.5 oz) cans green peas, drained
- 225g (1 cup) breadcrumbs

### INSTRUCTIONS

1. In a bowl, mix the condensed cream of mushroom soup, garlic powder, soured cream, ¾ cup of the cheddar cheese, and butter. Mix well and fold in the green peas.
2. Spread the mixture into a baking dish with a good size for your air fryer, then spread the remaining cheese on top.
3. Set the air fryer to 175°C (350°F) for 20 minutes.
4. Put the baking dish in the air fryer and bake for 15 to 20 minutes or until the cheese melts and is golden brown and the cream is bubbly.
5. Take out the dish, let it cool slightly and serve warm.

## SWEET POTATO FRIES

*Servings: 4*

**TOTAL CALORIES: 123**
Protein: 2.99g | Fats: 3.12g | Carbs: 21.85g

### INGREDIENTS

- 450g (1 lb) sweet potatoes
- 10 to 15g (2 to 3 tsp) melted butter
- 15g (1 tbsp) garlic granules
- Salt to taste
- Chopped fresh parsley for garnish

### INSTRUCTIONS

1. Peel the sweet potatoes and cut them into fries.
2. Add them to a bowl with the butter, garlic, and salt and toss them until properly coated.
3. Set the air fryer to 190°C (380°F) for 12 minutes.
4. Add the sweet potatoes to the air fryer basket and fry for 10 to 12 minutes or until they are golden brown and tender, shaking the basket 2 to 3 times during cooking.
5. Plate the parsnips, garnish them with parsley, and serve warm.

## SWEET ROASTED SWEDES

*Servings: 4*

**TOTAL CALORIES:66**
Protein: 1.07g | Fats: 3g | Carbs: 9.49 g

### INGREDIENTS

- 450g (1 lb) swedes
- 10 to 15ml (2 to 3 tsp) melted butter
- Salt to taste
- 10ml (2 tsp) maple syrup
- Chopped fresh parsley for garnish

### INSTRUCTIONS

1. Peel the swedes and cut them into thick chip shapes.
2. Add them to a bowl with the butter, salt, and maple syrup. Toss well.
3. Set the air fryer to 180°C (360°F) for 14 minutes.
4. Add the swedes to the air fryer basket and fry for 14 minutes or until they are golden brown while turning them halfway through cooking.
5. Remove the swedes onto serving plates, garnish them with parsley, and serve warm.

## YORKSHIRE PUDDING

*Servings: 4*

**TOTAL CALORIES:542**
Protein: 21.93g | Fats: 8.27g | Carbs: 92.06g

### INGREDIENTS

- 450g (2 cups) all-purpose flour / gluten-free flour
- 4 large eggs, cracked into a bowl
- 480ml (2 cups) milk
- 5g (1 tsp) salt
- Cooking spray

### INSTRUCTIONS

1. Mix the flour, eggs, milk, and salt until smooth.
2. Grease four medium ramekins with cooking spray and pour the batter into the ramekins halfway.
3. Place the ramekins in the air fryer basket.
4. Set the air fryer to 190°C (380°F) for 12 minutes.
5. Bake for 10 to 12 minutes or until the puddings have risen, are golden brown, and cooked through.
6. Take them out, let them cool slightly, and serve.

# WELSH ANGLESEY EGGS

*Servings: 4*

**TOTAL CALORIES: 722**
Protein: 32.53g | Fats: 43.36g | Carbs: 50.37g

## INGREDIENTS

For the mashed potatoes and eggs:
- 450g (1 lb) potatoes, peeled
- 50g (3¼ tbsp) butter, equally divided
- 30ml (2 tbsp) milk
- 1 large leek, trimmed, finely chopped, and well-rinsed
- Salt and black pepper to taste
- 8 hard-boiled eggs, peeled and quartered

For the sauce:
- 25g (1¾ tbsp) butter
- 50g (3¼ tbsp) plain flour
- 600ml (2½ cups) milk
- 150g (¾ cup) Caerphilly cheese, crumbled and equally divided
- Salt to taste

For the topping:
- 50g (3¼ tbsp) breadcrumbs

## INSTRUCTIONS

1. Boil the potatoes in salted boiling water until they are tender. Drain them well and pour them in a bowl. Add the half of the butter and milk, and mash them smoothly. Season with salt and black pepper.
2. Melt the remaining butter in a pan and sauté the leeks for 5 minutes or until they are tender. (You can do this while the potatoes cook). Mix the leek into the mashed potatoes.
3. Spread the mashed potatoes in a baking dish (that can fit into your air fryer) and arrange the quartered eggs on top.
4. Set the air fryer to 200°C (400°F) for 30 minutes.

For the sauce:
5. In the same pan that the potatoes cooked in, add the milk, flour, and butter. Cook over medium heat while whisking until smooth and thickened. Let simmer for 2 more minutes.
6. Add one part of the cheese and whisk until smooth. Season with salt.
7. Pour the sauce over the mashed potatoes.
8. Mix the remaining cheese with the breadcrumbs and spread it on top of the dish.

To bake:
9. Put the baking dish in the air fryer and bake for 15 to 20 minutes or until the dish is golden brown and bubbly.
10. Take out the dish and serve warm.

# 7 | SEAFOOD TO LOVE

*Seafood is perfectly quintessential and yet ready in nearly no time. Making them with the air fryer is so much fun. They absorb a lot of flavour, so if you're a seafood lover, you just might have found your best avenue to cook it perfectly.*

DON'T FORGET TO GET THE

**TOP RECIPES** FROM THIS BOOK AS

**A FREE DOWNLOADABLE PDF IN COLOUR**

**SCAN THE QR CODE BELOW**

*Just follow the steps below to access it via the QR Code (the picture code at the bottom of this page) or click the link if you are reading this on your Phone / Device.*

1. Unlock your phone & open up the phone's camera
2. Make sure you are using the "back" camera (as if you were taking a photo of someone) and point it towards the QR code at the bottom of the page.
3. Tap your phone's screen exactly where the QR code is.
4. A link / pop up will appear. Simply tap that (and make sure you have internet connection) and the FREE PDF containing all of the colored images should appear.

## BASIL PRAWNS

*Servings: 4*

**TOTAL CALORIES: 193**
Protein: 45.41g | Fats: 1.19g |
Carbs: 0.16g

### INGREDIENTS

- 900g (2 lb) prawns, peeled and deveined
- 240ml (1 cup) basil pesto
- Salt to taste
- Cooking spray

### INSTRUCTIONS

1. Add the prawns, pesto, and salt to a bowl. Toss them well.
2. Set the air fryer to 200°C (400°F) for 8 minutes.
3. Mist the air fryer basket with cooking spray and arrange the prawns in it. Mist the top again with cooking spray and bake for 4 minutes. Turn the prawns and cook for 4 more minutes or until they are pink and crispy at their edges.
4. Remove the prawns onto serving plates and serve them warm.

## BLACKENED SEA BASS

*Servings: 4*

**TOTAL CALORIES: 167**
Protein: 25.32g | Fats: 3.82g |
Carbs: 8.79g

### INGREDIENTS

- 30g (2 tbsp) paprika
- 5g (1 tsp) dried oregano
- 10g (2 tsp) brown sugar
- 5g (1 tsp) garlic powder
- 1g (¼ tsp) cayenne pepper
- 3g (½ tsp) ground cumin
- 5g (1 tsp) salt or to taste
- 4 (170g / 6 oz) sea bass fillets
- Cooking spray

### INSTRUCTIONS

1. In a small bowl, mix the paprika, oregano, brown sugar, garlic powder, cayenne pepper, cumin, and salt.
2. Rub the spice on both sides of the fish, making sure to cover well. Spray the fish with cooking spray and place them in the air fryer basket without overlapping.
3. Set the air fryer to 200°C (400°F) for 8 minutes.
4. Bake for 4 minutes per side or until the fish is golden brown with black patches all around, but not burnt.
5. Serve the fish warm.

# CRAB CAKES

*Servings: 4*
*Chill Time: 30 mins to 2 hours*

**TOTAL CALORIES: 140**
Protein: 6.73g | Fats: 3.38g |
Carbs: 21.27g

## INGREDIENTS

- 225g (8 oz) lump crab meat
- 2 salad onions, chopped
- 60g (¼ cup) chopped red bell pepper
- 30ml (2 tbsp) mayonnaise
- 5g (1 tsp) Old Bay seasoning
- 15ml (1 tbsp) English mustard
- 30g (2 tbsp) breadcrumbs
- Salt and black pepper to taste
- Cooking spray
- Lemon wedges for serving

## INSTRUCTIONS

1. In a bowl, mix the crab meat, salad onions, red bell pepper, mayonnaise, Old Bay seasoning, mustard, breadcrumbs, salt, and black pepper. Form the mixture into 4 equal patties and refrigerate for 30 minutes or up to 2 hours.
2. Set the air fryer to 188°C (375°F) for 12 minutes.
3. Grease the air fryer basket with cooking spray, place the patties in it and mist their tops with cooking spray.
4. Air fry them for 6 minutes per side or until they are

# CRAB-STUFFED SALMON

*Servings: 4*

**TOTAL CALORIES: 652**
Protein: 87.24g | Fats: 21.91g |
Carbs: 21.39g

## INGREDIENTS

- 225g (8 oz) fresh crab meat
- 60g (¼ cup) breadcrumbs
- 60g (2 oz) soft cheese, at room temperature
- 5ml (1 tsp) English mustard
- 15ml (1 tbsp) mayonnaise
- 5ml (1 tsp) hot sauce
- ½ lemon, juiced
- 30g (2 tbsp) chopped fresh parsley
- Salt and black pepper to taste
- 4 salmon fillets

## INSTRUCTIONS

1. Add the crab meat to a bowl and mix with the breadcrumbs, soft cheese, English mustard, mayonnaise, hot sauce, lemon juice, and parsley.
2. Cut a slit through the top of each salmon to about their middles. Season them with salt and black pepper. Stuff the salmon with the crab meat mixture all the way to the top and somewhat overflowing, then mist them with cooking spray.
3. Set the air fryer to 188°C (375°F) for 12 minutes.
4. Put the stuffed salmon in the air fryer basket without overlapping and bake for 10 to 12 minutes or until golden brown and flaky.
5. Plate the crab-stuffed salmon and serve warm.

## GINGERED TUNA STEAK

*Servings: 4*

### TOTAL CALORIES: 82
Protein: 12.01g | Fats: 1.81g | Carbs: 4.33g

### INGREDIENTS

- 60ml (¼ cup) soy sauce
- 3ml (½ tsp) rice vinegar
- 10g (2 tsp) grated fresh ginger
- 10ml (2 tsp) honey
- 5 tsp (1 tsp) sesame oil
- 4 (170g / 6 oz) yellowfin tuna steaks, boneless and skinless
- Sesame seeds for garnish
- Chopped green onions for garnish

### INSTRUCTIONS

1. In a large bowl, mix the soy sauce, rice vinegar, ginger, honey, and sesame oil. Place the tuna in the marinade, making sure to cover well with the marinade. Place the bowl in the refrigerator, cover, and marinate for 20 to 30 minutes.
2. Set the air fryer to 190°C (380°F) for 4 minutes.
3. Transfer the tuna from the marinade to the air fryer basket without overlapping and cook for 4 minutes.
4. Remove the tuna onto a slicing board and let rest for 1 to 2 minutes. Slice them and serve immediately.

## HERB AND CHILLI CALAMARI

*Servings: 4*

### TOTAL CALORIES: 314
Protein: 23.27g | Fats: 4.55g | Carbs: 44.34g

### INGREDIENTS

- 450g (1 lb) calamari or squid rings, cleaned
- 240ml (1 cup) milk
- 110g (½ cup) all-purpose flour / gluten-free flour
- 60g (¼ cup) arrowroot flour
- 5g (1 tsp) garlic powder
- 15g (1 tbsp) smoked paprika
- 3g (½ tsp) dried parsley
- 5g (1 tsp) cayenne pepper
- 3g (½ tsp) salt
- Cooking spray
- Chopped fresh parsley for garnish
- Red chilli flakes for garnish

### INSTRUCTIONS

1. Combine the calamari or squid and milk in a bowl, and let soak for 1 hour.
2. Meanwhile, in another bowl, mix both flours, garlic powder, paprika, parsley, cayenne pepper, and salt.
3. Drain the milk from the calamari and coat each one in the flour mixture while shaking off the excess flour.
4. Set the air fryer to 188°C (375°F) for 8 minutes.
5. Mist the air fryer basket with cooking spray, add the calamari, mist again with cooking spray and fry for 8 minutes, while flipping them halfway through cooking until they are golden brown.
6. Remove them onto a serving platter and garnish with the parsley and red chilli flakes.
7. Serve warm with your favourite dipping sauce.

# HONEY MUSTARD POLLOCK

*Servings: 4*

**TOTAL CALORIES: 110**
Protein: 9.71g | Fats: 3.95g |
Carbs: 9.11g

## INGREDIENTS

- 4 pollock fillets
- 1 tbsp olive oil
- Salt and black pepper to taste
- 30ml (2 tbsp) English mustard
- 30ml (2 tbsp) honey

## INSTRUCTIONS

1. Brush the pollock on both sides with olive oil and season with salt and black pepper. In a small bowl, mix the mustard and honey and brush the mixture on both sides of the fish.
2. Set the air fryer to 200°C (400°F) for 12 minutes.
3. Grease the air fryer with cooking spray and place the fish in it without overlapping. Bake for 10 to 12 minutes or until the fish is golden brown and flaky within.
4. Dish the pollock and serve warm.

# LEMON CAPER COD

*Servings: 4*

**TOTAL CALORIES: 110**
Protein: 18.02g | Fats: 3.43g |
Carbs: 1.03g

## INGREDIENTS

- 4 cod fillets
- Salt and black pepper to taste
- Cooking spray
- 20g (1½ tbsp) unsalted butter, melted
- 45ml (3 tbsp) fresh lemon juice
- 15g (1 tbsp) capers
- 3g (½ tsp) fresh lemon zest

## INSTRUCTIONS

1. Pat the dry cod with paper towels and season with salt and black pepper. Mist the cod on both sides with a little cooking spray.
2. Set the air fryer to 200°C (400°F) for 8 minutes.
3. Line the air fryer basket with foil and lay the cod in it. Bake them for 2 to 3 minutes per side.
4. Meanwhile, in a bowl, mix the butter, lemon juice, capers, and lemon zest.
5. Drizzle the mixture over the cod when ready and bake further for 2 minutes.
6. Carefully lift the cod onto serving plates and drizzle the capers butter on the foil on the fish.
7. Serve warm.

## LEMON GARLIC SALMON

*Servings: 4*

### TOTAL CALORIES: 275
Protein: 34.72g | Fats: 13.21g | Carbs: 2.65g

### INGREDIENTS

- 4 (6 oz) salmon fillets
- 30ml (2 tbsp) olive oil
- 10g (2 tsp) garlic powder
- Salt and black pepper to taste
- 1 lemon, sliced into thin rounds
- Chopped fresh dill for garnish

### INSTRUCTIONS

1. Pat the salmon fillets dry with paper towels and brush both sides with olive oil. Season with garlic powder, salt, and black pepper.
2. Set the air fryer to 200°C (400°F) for 12 minutes.
3. Lay the salmon in the air fryer and arrange the lemon slices on top. Bake for 10 to 12 minutes or until the salmon is flaky.
4. Garnish with some dill and serve warm.

## LOBSTER TAILS WITH LEMON-GARLIC BUTTER

*Servings: 4*

### TOTAL CALORIES: 162
Protein: 25.51g | Fats: 5.43g | Carbs: 1.89g

### INGREDIENTS

- 30g (2 tbsp) unsalted butter
- 3 garlic cloves, minced
- 15ml (1 tbsp) fresh lemon juice
- 30g (2 tbsp) chopped fresh parsley
- 3g (½ tsp) smoked paprika
- Salt and black pepper to taste
- 4 (110 to 170g / 4 to 6 oz) lobster tails
- Lemon wedges for serving

### INSTRUCTIONS

1. In a bowl, mix the butter, garlic, lemon juice, parsley, paprika, salt, and black pepper. Set it aside to develop its flavour.
2. Butterfly the lobster tails by using kitchen shears to cut their top hard shells lengthwise through the centre, making sure not to cut all the way through the bottom of the shell. Spread the shells open and use your fingers to gently pull the meat from inside the shell to the top of it. Remove any veins and dirt in them.
3. Season the lobster with a little salt and black pepper and then spread the lemon garlic butter on both sides of them.
4. Set the air fryer to 160°C (380°F) for 4 minutes.
5. Line the air fryer basket with foil and place the lobster tails in it. You can do this in batches. Cook for 4 minutes, baste the lobster tails with more lemon garlic butter and cook for 2 to 4 more minutes or until they are pink and meat opaque.
6. Remove the lobster tails onto a serving platter and serve warm with lemon wedges.

## 11 MACKEREL-STUFFED MUSHROOMS

*Servings: 4*

**(IN MINUTES)**
**PREP 10**
**COOK 15**

**TOTAL CALORIES: 333**
Protein: 22.36g | Fats: 22.11g | Carbs: 12.82g

### INGREDIENTS

- 4 large portabella mushrooms
- Cooking spray
- Salt and black pepper to taste
- 30g (2 tbsp) butter
- 1 small white onion, diced
- 2 garlic cloves, minced
- 3g (½ tsp) dried oregano
- 1g (¼ tsp) chilli flakes
- 3g (½ tsp) fennel seeds
- 1 (115g / 4 oz) can mackerel, drained
- 110g (½ cup) grated Old Winchester cheese
- 225g (1 cup) ricotta cheese
- 1 lemon, zested

### INSTRUCTIONS

1. Clean out the gills and stems from the mushrooms. Rinse them well and pat them dry with paper towels. Grease them with a bit of cooking spray and season with salt and black pepper. Put them aside.
2. Melt the butter in a pot and sauté the onion for 3 minutes or until they are tender. Stir in the garlic and cook for 1 minute or until fragrant. Stir in the oregano, chilli flakes, and fennel and cook for 1 minute or until fragrant. Turn the heat off and break in the mackerel. Mix along with the cheeses and lemon zest.
3. Spoon the mixture into the mushrooms, making sure to fill them to the very top.
4. Set the air fryer to 190°C (380°F) for 15 minutes.
5. Put the mushrooms in the air fryer and bake for 12 to 15 minutes or until they are tender and the cheese has melted.
6. Once ready, serve them warm.

## MIXED SEAFOOD PLATTER 12

*Servings: 4*

**TOTAL CALORIES: 83**
Protein: 15.38g | Fats: 1.17g | Carbs: 1.91g

**(IN MINUTES)**
**PREP 20**
**COOK 14**

### INGREDIENTS

- Cooking spray
- 450g (1 lb) frozen seafood mix
- Salt and black pepper to taste
- Chopped fresh parsley for garnish
- Lemon wedges for serving

### INSTRUCTIONS

1. Set the air fryer to 185°C (370°F) for 12 minutes.
2. Mist the air fryer basket with cooking spray and pour in the seafood mix. Mist the seafood mix with cooking spray.
3. Fry for 10 to 12 minutes while shaking the basket two to three times during cooking until the seafood is golden brown and cooked within but not rubbery.
4. Pour the seafood mix onto a serving platter, garnish with parsley and serve with lemon wedges.

# SCALLOP SUMMER SALAD

Servings: 4

**TOTAL CALORIES: 190**
Protein: 12.37g | Fats: 8.56g | Carbs: 19.25g

## INGREDIENTS

For the scallops:
- 225g (½ lb) scallops
- 3g (½ tsp) paprika
- 5g (1 tsp) lemon pepper, without salt
- Salt and black pepper to taste
- Cooking spray

For the basil vinaigrette:
- 60g (¼ cup) chopped fresh basil
- 30ml (2 tbsp) lemon juice
- 45ml (3 tbsp) white balsamic vinegar

- 30ml (2 tbsp) olive oil
- 10ml (2 tsp) English mustard
- Salt and black pepper to taste

For the salad:
- 1.5kg (6 cups) mixed salad greens, torn
- 1 medium red sweet pepper, seeded and chopped
- 3 tomatoes, seeded and chopped
- ½ medium English cucumber, chopped
- 1 cup canned corn kernels, drained

## INSTRUCTIONS

For the scallops:
1. Pat the scallops dry with a paper towel and season with the paprika, lemon pepper, salt, and black pepper.
2. Set the air fryer to 200°C (400°F) for 6 minutes.
3. Put the scallops in the air fryer basket in a single layer and fry for 3 minutes per side or until golden brown and opaque.

Meanwhile, prepare the basil vinaigrette:
4. In a blender, combine the basil, lemon juice, white balsamic vinegar, olive oil, mustard, salt, and black pepper. Blend until smooth.
5. Pour the vinaigrette into a serving jug.

For the salad:
6. In a large bowl, combine the salad greens, red sweet pepper, tomatoes, cucumber, and corn kernels. Drizzle on some of the dressing to your taste and toss well.
7. When the scallops are ready, add them to the salad and serve.

## SEASONED CRAB LEGS

*Servings: 4*

**TOTAL CALORIES: 129**
Protein: 22.83g | Fats: 3.95g | Carbs: 0.42g

### INGREDIENTS

- 1 cluster snow crab legs, fresh
- 30ml (2 tbsp) olive oil
- 15g (1 tbsp) Cajun seasoning

### INSTRUCTIONS

1. In a bowl, toss the crab legs with the olive oil and Cajun seasoning.
2. Set the air fryer to 175°C (350°F) for 5 minutes.
3. Arrange the crab legs in the air fryer basket and cook for 3 to 5 minutes or until pink on the shells.
4. Serve the crab legs with lemon wedges.

## SPICED BREADED HADDOCK

*Servings: 4*

**TOTAL CALORIES: 655**
Protein: 48.47g | Fats: 11.91g | Carbs: 85.34g

### INGREDIENTS

- 110g (½ cup) all-purpose flour / gluten-free flour
- 680g (3 cups) breadcrumbs
- 5g (1 tsp) paprika
- 3g (½ tsp) garlic powder
- 3g (½ tsp) chilli powder
- 1g (¼ tsp) ground cumin
- 2 eggs
- 90ml (6 tbsp) mayonnaise
- 4 (140g / 5 oz) haddock fillets
- Salt and black pepper to taste
- Lemon wedges for serving

### INSTRUCTIONS

1. Add the flour to a plate. On another plate, mix the breadcrumbs, paprika, garlic powder, chilli powder, and cumin. Crack the eggs into a bowl and whisk with the mayonnaise.
2. Pat dry the haddock with paper towels and season with salt and black pepper. Dredge them in the flour, dip them in the eggs, and coat them well in the spiced breadcrumbs.
3. Set the air fryer to 175°C (350°F) for 12 minutes.
4. Mist the air fryer basket with cooking spray, lay in the fish without overlapping, and mist again with cooking spray.
5. Bake the fish for 10 to 12 minutes or until they are golden brown and flaky within.
6. Plate the fish and serve warm with the lemon wedges.

## SWEET AND SOUR SHRIMP

*Servings: 4*

**TOTAL CALORIES: 245**
Protein: 23.75g | Fats: 0.63g | Carbs: 38.21g

### INGREDIENTS

- 120ml (½ cup) honey
- 30ml (2 tbsp) soy sauce, low-sodium
- 80ml (1/3 cup) rice vinegar
- 60ml (4 tbsp) pineapple juice
- 30g (2 tbsp) tomato puree
- 450g (1 lb) shrimp, peeled and deveined

### INSTRUCTIONS

1. In a bowl, mix the honey, soy sauce, rice vinegar, pineapple juice, and tomato puree. Add the shrimp and toss well.
2. Set the air fryer to 200°C (400°F) for 8 minutes.
3. Mist the air fryer basket with cooking spray and lay the shrimp in it. Mist the shrimp with cooking spray and cook for 6 to 8 minutes or until they are golden brown and opaque.
4. Plate the shrimp and serve warm.

## TILAPIA, POTATO, & SUN-DRIED TOMATO CASSEROLE

*Servings: 4*

**TOTAL CALORIES: 663**
Protein: 48.13g | Fats: 25.22g | Carbs: 68.11g

### INGREDIENTS

For the potatoes and fish:
- 450g (1 lb)) potatoes, peeled
- 450g (1 lb) tilapia fillets
- Salt and black pepper to taste
- 225g (1 cup) chopped sun dried tomatoes

For the sauce and topping:
- 600ml (2½ cup) milk
- 50g (3¾ tbsp) plain flour
- 25g (1¾ tbsp) butter
- 150g (5.3 oz) Caerphilly cheese, crumbled and equally divided
- Salt to taste

### INSTRUCTIONS

1. Peel the potatoes and using a mandolin, slice them very thinly. Also, cut the cod into small chunks. Season both the potatoes and fish with salt and black pepper. Set them aside.

For the sauce:

2. In a small pan, combine the milk, flour, and butter. Cook over medium heat while whisking until smooth and thickened. Let simmer for 2 more minutes.
3. Add one part of the cheese and whisk until smooth. Season with salt.

To bake:

4. Set the air fryer to 175°C (350°F) for 30 minutes.
5. In a baking dish that fits well in your air fryer, lay out a third each of the potatoes, fish, sun dried tomatoes, and the remaining cheese. Repeat the layering process two more times and pour the sauce all over it.
6. Put the baking dish in the air fryer and bake for 20 to 30 minutes or until the dish is golden brown and bubbly.
7. Take out the dish and serve warm.

# TUNA FISH CAKES

**18**

*Servings: 4*
*Chill Time: 30 mins to 2 hours*

**TOTAL CALORIES: 323**
Protein: 37.45g | Fats: 7.8g |
Carbs: 25.84g

## INGREDIENTS

- 2 (340g / 12 oz) cans of chunk tuna in water
- 2 eggs
- 110g (½ cup) seasoned breadcrumbs
- 60ml (4 tbsp) mayonnaise
- ½ white onion, diced
- 30ml (2 tbsp) fresh lemon juice
- Salt and black pepper to taste

## INSTRUCTIONS

1. Add the tuna to a bowl, crack in the eggs, and add the breadcrumbs, mayonnaise, white onion, lemon juice, salt, and black pepper. Mix the ingredients well and form into 4 equal patties. Refrigerate for 30 minutes or up to 2 hours.
2. When ready to cook, set the air fryer to 188°C (375°F) for 12 minutes.
3. Grease the air fryer basket with cooking spray, place the tuna patties in it and mist their tops with cooking spray.
4. Air fry them for 6 minutes per side or until they are golden brown and compacted.
5. Serve them warm with green salad.

# WHOLE FISH, ROASTED PEPPERS, & CARROTS PACKS

*Servings: 4*

**TOTAL CALORIES: 240**
Protein: 38.29g | Fats: 4.65g |
Carbs: 9.95g

## INGREDIENTS

- 1 (3 to 4 kg / 2 lb) whole fish
- 15ml (1 tbsp) olive oil
- Salt and black pepper to taste
- 1 (350g / 12 oz) roasted red pepper, drained and thinly sliced
- 2 carrots, cut into thin strips
- 1 white onion, sliced
- 15g (1 tbsp) chopped fresh dill
- 15g (1 tbsp) chopped fresh parsley

## INSTRUCTIONS

1. Cut out a large piece of foil that can wrap up the fish fully.
2. Lay the fish in the centre of the foil and spread the roasted red pepper, carrots, onion, dill, and parsley. Drizzle with olive oil and season with salt and black pepper. Wrap the foil over the fish and seal tightly.
3. Set the air fryer to 188°C (375°F) for 25 minutes.
4. Put the fish in the air fryer and bake for 20 to 25 minutes.
5. Serve the fish warm with rice, grains, or vegetables.

# SHRIMP FRIED RICE

*Servings: 4*

## TOTAL CALORIES: 405
Protein: 30.58g | Fats: 13.66g | Carbs: 39.55g

## INGREDIENTS

For the shrimp:
- 450g (1 lb) shrimp, peeled and deveined
- Salt and black pepper to taste
- 5g (1 tsp) corn starch

For the rice:
- 450g (2 cups) leftover cooked rice
- 225g (1 cup) frozen peas and carrots, defrosted
- 60g (¼ cup) chopped fresh green onions

- 45ml (3 tbsp) sesame oil
- 15ml (1 tbsp) soy sauce, low-sodium
- 3g (½ tsp) kosher salt
- 5g (1 tsp) black pepper

For the eggs:
- 2 large eggs
- Salt and black pepper to taste

## INSTRUCTIONS

For the shrimp:
1. Season the shrimp with salt and black pepper and toss them in the corn starch. Set them aside.

For the rice:
2. Set the air fryer to 175°C (350°F) for 25 minutes.
3. In a baking dish that fits into your air fryer, mix the rice, peas and carrots, green onions, soy sauce, sesame oil, and a little salt and black pepper.
4. Place the dish in the air fryer and cook for 15 minutes while stirring the rice after 8 minutes of cooking.
5. Place the shrimp on the rice and cook for 5 minutes.
6. Meanwhile, as the shrimp cooks, crack the eggs into a bowl and whisk with a pinch of salt and black pepper. Drizzle the eggs over the rice and cook for 5 minutes. Stir after.
7. Dish the shrimp fried rice and serve warm.

# 8 | HEALTHY WHITE & RED MEATS

*Did you know the air fryer cooks meat in a shorter time than the oven? And if you're looking for the best crisps on your steaks, chicken, etc., then this assemblage of lunch and dinner-worthy meat dishes would suit you.*

DON'T FORGET TO GET THE

**TOP RECIPES** FROM THIS BOOK AS

**A FREE DOWNLOADABLE PDF IN COLOUR**

**SCAN THE QR CODE BELOW**

*Just follow the steps below to access it via the QR Code (the picture code at the bottom of this page) or click the link if you are reading this on your Phone / Device.*

1. Unlock your phone & open up the phone's camera
2. Make sure you are using the "back" camera (as if you were taking a photo of someone) and point it towards the QR code at the bottom of the page.
3. Tap your phone's screen exactly where the QR code is.
4. A link / pop up will appear. Simply tap that (and make sure you have internet connection) and the FREE PDF containing all of the colored images should appear.

## BEEF PUFFS

*Servings: 4*

**TOTAL CALORIES: 1000**
Protein: 58.77g | Fats: 57.34g |
Carbs: 62.85g

### INGREDIENTS

- 450g (1 lb) beef mince
- ½ cup chopped onion
- ½ cup diced carrot
- 60g (¼ cup) canned garden peas, drained
- Salt and black pepper to taste
- 5g (1 tsp) garlic powder
- 3g (½ tsp) dried rosemary
- 15ml (1 tbsp) Worcestershire sauce
- 2 tubes (227g / 16.3 oz each) large refrigerated flaky biscuits
- 450g (2 cups) shredded cheddar cheese

### INSTRUCTIONS

1. Grease a skillet with cooking spray and cook the beef mince over medium heat for 5 minutes while stirring and breaking the lumps that form. Add the onion, carrot, and peas and cook for 5 minutes. Season with salt, black pepper, garlic powder, rosemary, and Worcestershire sauce. Turn the heat off.
2. Flatten half of the biscuits and cut out 8 (10cm / 4-inch) circles. On four of the circles, spoon a quarter each of the beef mixture on top and then a quarter each of the cheddar cheese on top. Cover with the other four pastries and crimp their edges. Use a knife to cut a slit at the centre of each.
3. Set the air fryer to 175°C (350°F) for 15 minutes.
4. Mist the air fryer basket with cooking spray, place in the beef pastries, and bake for 10 to 15 minutes or until they are golden brown and puffed up.
5. Put them on a plate, let them cool slightly, and serve.

## BEEF WELLINGTON

*Servings: 4*

**TOTAL CALORIES: 229**
Protein: 16.43g | Fats: 14.31g |
Carbs: 9.58g

### INGREDIENTS

- 15ml (1 tbsp) olive oil
- 2 (150 g) beef eye filet steaks
- 200g (1 cup) button mushrooms, finely chopped
- 2 shallots, peeled and finely chopped
- 2 garlic cloves, crushed
- 7 slices prosciutto
- 10ml (2 tsp) Dijon mustard
- 1 sheet frozen puff pastry, just thawed
- 1 egg, lightly whisked

### INSTRUCTIONS

1. Heat the olive oil in a skillet and cook the steaks for 1 to 2 minutes per side or until seared all around. Place the steaks on a plate and let cool slightly in the fridge.
2. Reduce the heat to low and sauté the shallots, mushrooms, and garlic in the same skillet for 15 minutes or until the liquid has evaporated and they are golden brown. Also, transfer them to a plate and let cool in the fridge to slightly cool.
3. Lay out a large plastic wrap, lay the 6 prosciutto slices on top while slightly overlapping to form a rectangle, and spread the mushroom mixture on top. Set the steaks on top following each other lengthwise and spread the mustard on top. Wrap the prosciutto over the steaks, place the last prosciutto on top to cover any gaps, and tuck the ends in. Cover tightly with the plastic wrap and place in the fridge for 20 minutes.
4. Lay the pastry on a clean flat surface, unwrap the meat log and set at the centre of the pastry. Fold the pastry over and tuck the seams to close. Place the seam side down and brush the top with egg. Then, use a knife to score 2 to 3 diagonal lines on top.
5. Set the air fryer to 180°C (360°F) for 20 minutes.
6. Place the wrapped meat in the air fryer basket and bake for 20 minutes or until golden brown and crispy.
7. Transfer to a chopping board and let rest for 10 minutes before slicing.
8. Serve warm with onion relish, gravy, or other sauces of choice.

## BEEF, BRIE, & ON-ION RELISH BURGER

(IN MINUTES)
PREP 10
COOK 8

*Servings: 4*

**TOTAL CALORIES: 407**
Protein: 35.42g | Fats: 18.03g | Carbs: 25.92g

### INGREDIENTS

For the beef patties:
- 450g (1 lb) beef mince
- 5g (1 tsp) onion powder
- 5g (1 tsp) garlic powder
- Salt and black pepper to taste
- Cooking spray
- 4 slices brie cheese

To assemble:
- 4 hamburger buns, split and toasted
- 4 lettuce leaves
- 240ml (1 cup) onion relish

### INSTRUCTIONS

For the beef patties:
1. In a bowl, mix all the ingredients until well combined. Form 4 patties from the mixture.
2. Set the air fryer to 190°C (375°F) for 15 minutes.
3. Mist the air fryer basket with cooking spray and place the beef patties in it. Cook for 7 to 8 minutes per side or until they are golden brown and reach an internal temperature of 63°C (145°F).
4. Transfer the beef patties to a plate and immediately lay one brie cheese on each one to melt while they rest for 10 minutes.

To assemble the burgers:
5. On the bottom parts of each hamburger bun, add one lettuce leaf and top with a beef-cheese patty each. Spoon the onion relish on top.
6. Then, cover up with the top buns and serve.

## CHEESY BEEF BALLS

(IN MINUTES)
PREP 15
COOK 12

*Servings: 4*

**TOTAL CALORIES: 423**
Protein: 9.42g | Fats: 6.65g | Carbs: 6.9g

### INGREDIENTS

- 450g (1 lb) beef mince
- 170g (¾ cup) plain breadcrumbs
- 3g (½ tsp) garlic powder
- 120ml (½ cup) milk
- 120ml (½ cup) BBQ sauce
- 1 egg, beaten
- Salt and black pepper to taste
- 12 to 15 small cheddar cheese cubes

### INSTRUCTIONS

1. In a bowl, mix the beef mince, breadcrumbs, garlic powder, milk, BBQ sauce, egg, salt, and black pepper. Form 12 to 15 balls from the mixture.
2. Press a hole into one meatball and place a cheese cube at the centre. Mould the meat around the cheese and do the same for the remaining meatballs.
3. Set the air fryer to 175°C (350°F) for 12 minutes.
4. Mist the air fryer with cooking spray and arrange the meatballs in it. Grease the meatballs with a little cooking spray too and cook for 10 to 12 minutes while shaking the basket 2 to 3 times during cooking.
5. Plate the beef balls and serve them with pasta or your favourite sauces.

## CHICKEN AND PINEAPPLE SKEWERS

*Servings: 4*

**TOTAL CALORIES: 134**
Protein: 2.53g | Fats: 5.33g | Carbs: 9.56g

### INGREDIENTS

- 225g (8 oz) chicken breasts, skinless and boneless
- Salt and black pepper to taste
- 225g (1 cup) pineapple chunks, 3cm (1-inch) pieces
- 120ml (4 oz) BBQ sauce, your favourite
- Air fryer skewers for threading

### INSTRUCTIONS

1. Season the chicken with salt and black pepper.
2. On your skewers, alternately thread the chicken and pineapple. Brush them with some of the BBQ sauce.
3. Set the air fryer to 200°C (400°F) for 12 minutes.
4. Place the skewers in the air fryer in a single layer and cook for 6 minutes. Brush the skewers with more BBQ sauce and cook further for 6 minutes or until they are golden brown.
5. Plate the skewers and let them rest for 5 minutes before serving.

## CHICKEN BREASTS WITH PORK SCRATCHINGS

*Servings: 4*

**TOTAL CALORIES: 521**
Protein: 41.56g | Fats: 36.49g | Carbs: 5.61g

### INGREDIENTS

For the marinade:
- 30ml (2 tbsp) plain yoghurt
- 10g (2 tsp) garlic paste
- 10g (2 tsp) ginger paste
- 10g (2 tsp) chilli powder
- 5g (1 tsp) paprika
- 5g (1 tsp) salt or to taste
- 4 chicken thighs, bone-in and skinless

For the pork scratchings crust:
- 110g (4 oz) pork scratchings, crushed
- 10g (2 tsp) grated Parmesan cheese
- 10 (2 tsp) paprika
- 10 (2 tsp) chilli powder

### INSTRUCTIONS

To marinate the chicken:
1. In a bowl, combine the yoghurt, garlic paste, ginger paste, chilli powder, paprika, and salt. Mix well and add the chicken to cover. Let marinate in the fridge for 30 minutes.

For the pork scratchings crust:
2. In a food processor, crush the pork scratchings along with the Parmesan cheese, paprika, and chilli powder until smooth. Pour the mixture onto a plate.
3. Remove the chicken from the marinade and coat it generously with the pork mixture.
4. Set the air fryer to 200°C (400°F) for 12 minutes.
5. Mist the air fryer basket with cooking spray and lay the chicken in it. Bake for 6 minutes per side or until the thickest part of the chicken reaches an internal temperature of 74°C (165°F).
6. Plate the chicken, let rest for 5 minutes, and then serve.

## CRISPY GOLDEN CUTLETS

*Servings: 4*

**TOTAL CALORIES: 263**
Protein: 31.97g | Fats: 4.53g | Carbs: 21.11g

### INGREDIENTS

- 2 large chicken breasts
- 60ml (¼ cup) egg whites
- 170g (¾ cup) seasoned breadcrumbs
- Cooking spray

### INSTRUCTIONS

1. Slice the chicken breasts in halves lengthwise, wrap them in cling film, and gently roll them with a rolling pin until flat.
2. Coat them in the egg whites and dress them well with the breadcrumbs.
3. Set the air fryer to 200°C (400°F) for 15 minutes.
4. Grease the air fryer basket with cooking spray, lay in the chicken, and grease the chicken with a bit of cooking spray. Bake them for 7 to 8 minutes per side or until they are golden brown, crispy, and reach an internal temperature of 74°C (165°F).
5. Plate the chicken, let them rest for 5 minutes, and then serve them with your favourite sauce.

## EXTRA CRUNCHY CHICKEN BREASTS

*Servings: 4*

**TOTAL CALORIES: 871**
Protein: 84.73g | Fats: 41.65g | Carbs: 39.42g

### INGREDIENTS

- 120ml (½ cup) whole buttermilk
- 60ml (4 tbsp) English mustard
- 4 (170g / 6 oz) chicken breasts, skinless and boneless
- 225g (1 cup) breadcrumbs
- 90g (6 tbsp) grated Old Winchester cheese
- 150g (2/3 cup) finely chopped pecans
- 8g (1½ tsp) finely chopped fresh rosemary
- 5g (1 tsp) kosher salt
- 3g (½ tsp) black pepper
- Cooking spray

### INSTRUCTIONS

1. Mix the buttermilk and mustard in a bowl. Add the chicken to the mixture and cover well.
2. On a plate, mix the breadcrumbs, Old Winchester cheese, pecans, rosemary, salt, and black pepper.
3. Remove the chicken from the buttermilk mixture and coat well in the bread crumb mixture.
4. Set the air fryer to 200°C (400°F) for 12 minutes.
5. Grease the air fryer basket with cooking spray and lay in the chicken. Mist again and cook for 6 minutes per side or until the thickest part of the chicken reaches an internal temperature of 74°C (165°F).
6. Take out the chicken and serve warm.

# LAMB HARISSA BURGER

*Servings: 4*

**TOTAL CALORIES: 544**
Protein: 36.14g | Fats: 25.77g | Carbs: 43.17g

## INGREDIENTS

**For the lamb patties:**
- 450g (1 lb) lamb mince
- ½ medium yellow onion, diced
- 3 garlic cloves, minced
- 5g (1 tsp) dried oregano
- 4g (¾ tsp) salt or to taste
- 3g (½ tsp) ground cumin

**For the harissa mayonnaise:**
- 60ml (¼ cup) mayonnaise
- 8g (1½ tsp) harissa powder

**To assemble:**
- 4 hamburger buns, split and toasted
- 225g (1 cup) baby rocket
- 110g (½ cup) fresh parsley leaves
- 4 large red onion rings
- Harissa mayonnaise

## INSTRUCTIONS

**For the lamb patties:**
1. In a bowl, mix all the ingredients until well combined. Form 4 patties from the mixture.
2. Set the air fryer to 190°C (375°F) for 15 minutes.
3. Mist the air fryer basket with cooking spray and place the lamb patties in it. Cook for 7 to 8 minutes per side or until they are golden brown and reach an internal temperature of 63°C (145°F).
4. Transfer the lamb patties to a plate to rest for 10 minutes.

**For the harissa mayonnaise:**
5. In a bowl, mix the mayonnaise and harissa powder until smooth.

**To assemble the burgers:**
6. On the bottom parts of the hamburger buns, divide the arugula to your taste and place one lamb patty on each. Top with the parsley, red onion, and drizzle on the harissa mayonnaise.
7. Cover up with the top buns and serve.

## NEW ENGLAND LAMB BAKE

*Servings: 4*

(IN MINUTES)
PREP 10
COOK 30

**TOTAL CALORIES: 1017**
Protein: 93.59g | Fats: 37.97g
| Carbs: 71.98 g

### INGREDIENTS

- 1 tbsp canola oil
- 900g (2 lb) boneless leg of lamb, cut into 3cm (1-inch) cubes
- 1 large onion, chopped
- 60g (¼ cup) plain flour
- 720ml (3 cups) chicken broth
- 2 large leeks (white portion only), cut into (1cm / ½-inch slices)
- 2 large carrots, sliced
- 1g (¼ tsp) dried thyme
- 30g (2 tbsp) minced fresh parsley, divided
- 3g (½ tsp) dried rosemary, crushed
- 3g (½ tsp) salt
- 1g (¼ tsp) black pepper
- 3 large potatoes, peeled and thinly sliced
- 45ml (3 tbsp) butter, melted, divided

### INSTRUCTIONS

1. Heat the canola oil in a skillet and cook the lamb and onion for 8 to 10 minutes or until the meat is no longer pink. Stir in the flour until well combined and gradually mix in the chicken broth until smooth sauce forms. Bring to a boil until the sauce thickens while stirring to loosen any stuck brown bits. Add the leeks, carrots, thyme, half of the parsley, rosemary, salt, and black pepper.
2. Spoon the mixture into a baking dish (that can fit into your air fryer) and arrange the potatoes on top in a single layer while slightly overlapping. Brush the potatoes with the butter.
3. Set the air fryer to 190°C (375°F) for 30 minutes.
4. Place the dish in the air fryer and bake for 25 to 30 minutes or until the potatoes are golden brown and tender.
5. Take out the dish, garnish with the remaining parsley, and serve warm.

## PARMO

*Servings: 4*

(IN MINUTES)
PREP 10
COOK 13

**TOTAL CALORIES: 489**
Protein: 46.87g | Fats: 4.93g |
Carbs: 37.45g

### INGREDIENTS

- 2 large boneless chicken breasts
- Salt and black pepper to taste
- 45g (3 tbsp) plain flour
- 2 large eggs
- 110g (½ cup) panko breadcrumbs
- 5g (1 tsp) dried oregano
- 3g (½ tsp) garlic powder
- 25g (1¾ tbsp) grated Parmesan
- 3g (½ tsp) chilli flakes
- 240g (¾ cup) tomato sauce
- 100g (½ cup) grated mozzarella
- Chopped fresh parsley for garnish

### INSTRUCTIONS

1. Slice the chicken lengthwise into equal halves and season with salt and black pepper.
2. Add the flour to a plate, beat the eggs in a bowl, and on another plate, mix the breadcrumbs, oregano, garlic powder, Parmesan, and chilli flakes.
3. Dredge the chicken in the flour, dip them in the eggs, and coat well with the breadcrumb mixture.
4. Set the air fryer to 200°C (400°F) for 13 minutes.
5. Mist the air fryer basket with cooking spray and lay the chicken in it. Mist the chicken with cooking spray and bake them for 5 minutes per side or until they are golden brown, crispy, and reach an internal temperature of 74°C (165°F).
6. After, spoon the tomato sauce on each chicken and carefully spread it out to coat their tops. Also, top them with the mozzarella cheese.
7. Bake for 3 more minutes or until the cheese melts.
8. Plate the chicken, garnish with parsley, and let them rest for 5 minutes before serving.

# PORK AND CHEESE-STUFFED COURGETTES

*Servings: 4*

## TOTAL CALORIES: 641
Protein: 39.05g | Fats: 51.99g | Carbs: 3.18g

## INGREDIENTS

- 2 large courgettes
- 450g (1 lb) pork mince
- 1 garlic clove, minced
- 170g (¾ cup) crumbled feta cheese, divided
- 225g (1 cup) shredded cheddar cheese
- 30g (2 tbsp) chopped fresh basil
- Salt and black pepper to taste
- Cooking spray

## INSTRUCTIONS

1. Cut the courgettes in halves lengthwise and scoop out their flesh to create a boat. Set the courgette boats aside. Chop the courgette flesh and add to a bowl.
2. Cook the pork mince in a skillet over medium heat for 10 minutes. Stir in the garlic, season with salt and black pepper, and cook for 2 more minutes.
3. Spoon the pork into the bowl with the courgette flesh and add half of the feta cheese, cheddar cheese, basil, salt, and black pepper. Mix well and spoon the mixture into the courgette boats.
4. Set the air fryer to 175°C (350°F) for 8 minutes.
5. Grease the air fryer basket with cooking spray and carefully set the stuffed courgettes in the basket. Add the remaining feta cheese on top and bake for 6 to 8 minutes or until the cheese melts.
6. Transfer the courgettes to a plate and serve warm.

# PORK CHOPS WITH CREAMY HERB SAUCE

*Servings: 4*

## TOTAL CALORIES: 376
Protein: 49.53g | Fats: 14.52g | Carbs: 7.23g

## INGREDIENTS

For the pork chops:
- 4 bone-in pork chops
- 30ml (2 tbsp) extra-virgin olive oil
- 5g (1 tsp) onion powder
- 10g (2 tsp) garlic powder
- 5g (1 tsp) smoked paprika
- 5g (1 tsp) ground mustard
- 3g (½ tsp) mixed herb seasoning
- 5g (1 tsp) salt or to taste
- 3g (½ tsp) freshly ground black pepper

For the creamy herb dressing:
- 45ml (3 tbsp) dry white wine
- 160ml (2/3 cup) chicken broth
- 8g (½ tbsp) corn starch
- 30ml (2 tbsp) soured cream
- 15ml (1 tbsp) coarse-grain mustard
- 5g (1 tsp) chopped fresh thyme

## INSTRUCTIONS

For the pork chops:
1. Rub the pork chops on both sides with olive oil and set aside.
2. In a bowl, mix the onion powder, garlic powder, paprika, mustard, mixed herb seasoning, salt, and black pepper. Rub the pork on both sides with the seasoning.
3. Set the air fryer to 200°C (400°F) for 12 minutes.
4. Lay the pork chops in the air fryer basket and cook for 6 minutes per side or until golden brown and reaches an internal temperature of 63°C (145°F).
5. Remove the pork chops onto a platter and let them rest for 10 minutes.

For the creamy herb sauce:
6. In a saucepan, whisk the wine, broth, and corn starch. Cook over low heat while stirring until thickened.
7. Stir in the soured cream, mustard, and thyme until well-combined. Simmer for 1 to 2 minutes and turn the heat off.
8. Spoon the sauce over the pork chops and serve warm.

## PUB STEAK WITH PARSLEY TOPPING

*Servings: 4*

**TOTAL CALORIES: 1331**
Protein: 82.17g | Fats: 11.18g | Carbs: 1.46g

## INGREDIENTS

For the pub steak:
- 4 (3cm / 1-inch) rib eye steak
- 15ml (1 tbsp) olive oil
- 5g (1 tsp) mixed herb seasoning
- Salt and black pepper to taste

For the parsley butter topping:
- 60g (¼ cup) butter, at room temperature
- 1 garlic clove, minced
- 30g (2 tbsp) chopped fresh parsley

## INSTRUCTIONS

For the pub steak:
1. Set the air fryer to 200°C (400°F) for 12 minutes.
2. Rub the steaks with the olive oil on each side and season with the mixed herbs, salt, and black pepper.
3. Place the steaks in the air fryer basket and cook for 6 minutes per side for medium.
4. Transfer the steak to a platter to rest for 10 minutes.

For the parsley butter topping:
5. Mix the butter, garlic, and parsley in a bowl and spoon over the steaks.
6. Serve warm.

## ROASTED LAMB WITH GARDEN RUB

*Servings: 4*

**TOTAL CALORIES: 423**
Protein: 41.93g | Fats: 2.18g | Carbs: 18.62g

## INGREDIENTS

For the lamb:
- 1 rack of lamb, dressed
- 15ml (1 tbsp) olive oil

For the garden rub:
- 375g (1 1/3 cups) coarse sea salt
- 60g (¼ cup) coarse ground black pepper
- 30g (2 tbsp) garlic powder
- 150g (2/3 cup) dried parsley
- 60g (¼ cup) dried rosemary, crushed
- 75g (1/3 cup) dried thyme
- 60g (¼ cup) dried shredded lemon peel
- 30g (2 tbsp) dried minced onion

## INSTRUCTIONS

1. Rub the rack of lamb on both sides with olive oil and set aside.
2. In a bowl, mix the salt, black pepper, garlic powder, parsley, rosemary, thyme, lemon peel, and dried onion. Rub the lamb on both sides with the seasoning.
3. Set the air fryer to 200°C (400°F) for 22 minutes.
4. Place the lamb in the air fryer basket and cook for 18 to 22 minutes per side or to your desired doneness.
5. Remove the lamb onto a platter and let it rest for 10 minutes before slicing and serving.

## ROSEMARY GARLIC LAMB CHOPS

*Servings: 4*

### TOTAL CALORIES: 829
Protein: 37.08g | Fats: 73.68g | Carbs: 2.6g

### INGREDIENTS

- 900g (2 lb) lamb chops
- 60ml (¼ cup) olive oil
- 1 lemon, zested
- 15g (1 tbsp) chopped fresh rosemary
- 4 garlic cloves, minced
- Salt and black pepper to taste
- Fresh rosemary sprigs for garnish

### INSTRUCTIONS

1. Put the lamb chops in a bowl.
2. In a small bowl, mix the olive oil, lemon zest, rosemary, garlic, salt, and black pepper. Pour the mixture over the lamp and let it marinate for 15 minutes.
3. Set the air fryer to 200°C (400°F) for 12 minutes.
4. Remove the lamb from the marinade, drip off the marinade, and place them in the air fryer basket.
5. Cook for 6 minutes per side or until they are golden brown and reach an internal temperature of 63°C (145°F).
6. Remove the lamb chops onto a platter and let them rest for 10 minutes.
7. Garnish with rosemary sprigs and serve warm.

## STEAK, ALE, & CARAMELIZED ONION PIE

*Servings: 4*

### TOTAL CALORIES: 1180
Protein: 94.38g | Fats: 61.39g | Carbs: 63.66g

### INGREDIENTS

- 30ml (2 tbsp) vegetable oil
- 1 kg (2 lb) braising steak, cut into 3cm chunks
- Salt and black pepper to taste
- 3 large onions, thinly sliced
- 4 large carrots, chopped into large chunks
- 10g (2 tsp) golden caster sugar
- 60g (4 tbsp) plain or all-purpose flour
- 300ml (1 and 1/3 cup) dark ale
- 2 beef stock cubes mixed with 400ml (1¾ cup) boiling water
- A small bunch each bay leaf, thyme, and parsley
- 225g (1 cup) smoked bacon lardons, chopped
- 1 large refrigerated pie crust
- 1 egg, beaten

### INSTRUCTIONS

1. Heat 1 tablespoon of oil in a pot over medium heat. Season the beef with salt and black pepper and sear in the oil for 2 to 3 minutes per side or until light brown. Remove them onto a plate and set them aside.
2. Reduce the heat to low and sauté the onion for 10 to 15 minutes or until they are caramelized. Add the carrots and sauté for 5 minutes or until tender. Stir in the sugar and flour, and cook until the flour turns brown.
3. Gradually mix in the dark ale and beef stock, return the beef and any drippings to the pot, add the tied herbs, and season with salt and black pepper. Cover with a lid and cook over the least heat for 45 minutes to 1 hour.
4. After the stew cooks, add the bacon to a pan and cook for 3 minutes or until crispy. Stir the bacon into the stew and discard the tied herbs.
5. Spoon the stew into a pie pan (good for your air fryer) and spread the pie crust on top of it; crimp the edges. Brush the top with the egg and use a knife to cut a slit or two on top.
6. Set the air fryer to 200°C (400°F) for 40 minutes.
7. Place the pie pan into the air fryer and bake for 40 minutes or until the crust is golden brown and the filling is bubbly.
8. Put the pie pan on a heat proof surface and let cool slightly before serving.

## 18  THAT SPICY CHICK-EN DRUMETTES

*Servings: 4*

**TOTAL CALORIES: 263**
Protein: 20.04g | Fats: 18.89g | Carbs: 3.08g

### INGREDIENTS

- 12 chicken wings
- 15ml (1 tbsp) olive oil
- 5g (1 tsp) baking powder
- 5g (1 tsp) garlic powder
- 60ml (¼ cup) melted butter
- 240ml (1 cup) hot sauce, extra spicy
- 3g (½ tsp) salt
- 5g (1 tsp) ground black pepper

### INSTRUCTIONS

1. Split the chicken in the middle into two pieces and place them in a bowl. Add the olive oil, baking powder, and garlic powder. Toss well.
2. Set the air fryer to 190°C (380°F) for 20 minutes.
3. Arrange the chicken in the air fryer basket and cook for 20 minutes while turning them every 5 minutes or until they are golden brown.
4. Meanwhile, in a bowl, mix the butter, hot sauce, salt, and black pepper.
5. Transfer the ready chicken to the bowl and toss to coat well.
6. Plate the chicken and serve warm.

## 19  VEGGIE TURKEY MEATLOAF

*Servings: 4*

**TOTAL CALORIES: 454**
Protein: 31.4g | Fats: 10.56g | Carbs: 65.23g

### INGREDIENTS

- 450g (1 lb) turkey mince
- 1 small onion, finely diced
- 1 green pepper, deseeded and finely chopped
- 1 medium carrot, finely diced
- 2 garlic cloves, finely minced
- 3g (½ tsp) granulated garlic
- 5g (1 tsp) mixed herb seasoning
- 1 egg, cracked into a bowl
- A pinch of red pepper flakes
- 60ml (¼ cup) ketchup
- 5ml (1 tsp) Worcestershire sauce
- 15g (1 tbsp) brown sugar
- 10 plain flavoured crackers, crushed
- Salt and black pepper to taste
- 240ml (1 cup) tomato sauce

### INSTRUCTIONS

1. Line a loaf pan (good for your air fryer) with foil with a bit of it falling over the loaf pan for lifting the meatloaf when ready.
2. Add all the ingredients to a bowl except for the tomato sauce and mix them well. Spoon the turkey mix into the loaf pan and mould to fit the shape of the loaf pan. Spread the tomato sauce on top.
3. Set the air fryer to 175°C (350°F) for 20 minutes.
4. Place the loaf pan in the air fryer and bake for 18 to 20 minutes or until the meat is longer pink within.
5. Take out the loaf pan and let the meatloaf rest in it for 10 minutes. Carefully, hold the hanging sides of the foil and lift the meatloaf onto a serving platter.
6. Slice and serve warm.

# WILD DUCK WITH FIGS & CRANBERRIES

Servings: 4

**TOTAL CALORIES: 555**
Protein: 22.26g | Fats: 24.86g | Carbs: 62.57g

## INGREDIENTS

For the wild duck:
- 2 wild duck breasts, boneless
- Salt and black pepper to taste

For the fig and cranberry sauce:
- 45g (3 tbsp) unsalted butter
- 1 large shallot, finely chopped
- 15g (1 tbsp) finely chopped rosemary
- 170g (6 oz) dried figs, coarsely chopped
- 450g (1 lb) fresh or frozen cranberries
- 60ml (¼ cup) balsamic vinegar
- 150g (2/3 cup) light brown sugar, packed
- Salt to taste
- A pinch of red pepper flakes
- Fresh rosemary sprigs for garnish

## INSTRUCTIONS

For the wild duck:
1. Score the skin of the duck breasts and season both sides with salt and black pepper.
2. Set the air fryer to 195°C (390°F) for 5 minutes.
3. Place the duck breasts with skin side up and cook for 5 minutes. Reduce the heat to 160°C (320°F) for 10 to 12 minutes or until the skins are golden brown and the duck reaches an internal temperature of 74°C/165°F.
4. Remove them onto a plate and tent them with foil for 10 minutes.

For the fig and cranberry sauce:
5. Meanwhile, melt the butter in a saucepan and sauté the shallots for 2 minutes or until tender.
6. Add the rosemary, figs, cranberries, balsamic vinegar, brown sugar, and salt. Stir and cook for 5 minutes or until the figs and cranberries break and the sauce thickens.
7. Add the red pepper flakes and stir through.
8. Slice the duck and plate them.
9. Spoon the sauce over the duck, garnish with rosemary sprigs, and serve.

# 9 | YUMMY VEGETARIAN & VEGAN DISHES

*A good vegetable toss, bake, or roast is something to enjoy on a warm evening. Indulging in the freshness of veggies topped with other non-meaty foods is a great way to switch up my diet for versatility. Here, I share some of my favourite vegetarian and vegan foods to enjoy with your air fryer. You also do not need to be vegan to enjoy them. They are for everyone.*

## DON'T FORGET TO GET THE
## **TOP RECIPES** FROM THIS BOOK
## AS
## A FREE DOWNLOADABLE PDF IN COLOUR

### SCAN THE QR CODE BELOW

*Just follow the steps below to access it via the QR Code (the picture code at the bottom of this page) or click the link if you are reading this on your Phone / Device.*

1. Unlock your phone & open up the phone's camera
2. Make sure you are using the "back" camera (as if you were taking a photo of someone) and point it towards the QR code at the bottom of the page.
3. Tap your phone's screen exactly where the QR code is.
4. A link / pop up will appear. Simply tap that (and make sure you have internet connection) and the FREE PDF containing all of the colored images should appear.

# ALMONDS AND BROCCOLI

*Servings: 4*

**TOTAL CALORIES: 142**
Protein: 5.16g | Fats: 9.94g | Carbs: 11.49g

## INGREDIENTS

- 1 head broccoli, separated into florets
- 30g (2 tbsp) olive oil
- 3g (½ tsp) onion powder
- Salt and black pepper to taste
- 15g (1 tbsp) sliced toasted almonds for topping

## INSTRUCTIONS

1. Set the air fryer to 180°C (360°F) for 12 minutes.
2. In a bowl, toss the broccoli, olive oil, salt, and black pepper.
3. Add the broccoli to the air fryer basket and roast for 10 to 12 minutes or until golden brown and tender, while shaking the basket once or twice during cooking.
4. Remove the broccoli into a bowl, sprinkle the almonds on top, and serve warm.

# BBQ SOY CURLS

*Servings: 4*

**TOTAL CALORIES: 99**
Protein: 15.45g | Fats: 0.64g | Carbs: 9.8g

## INGREDIENTS

- 675g (3 cups) soy curls
- 960ml (4 cups) boiling water
- 15ml (1 tbsp) Dijon mustard
- 8ml (1½ tsp) BBQ sauce, your favourite type

## INSTRUCTIONS

1. Add the soy curls to a bowl and pour on the boiling water. Let them soak and hydrate for 10 minutes. Drain them after and set a heavy bowl on them to press out more moisture. With the bowl still on them, drain the excess liquid.
2. Remove the heavy bowl and stir the Dijon mustard and BBQ sauce through them.
3. Set the air fryer to 200°C (400°F) for 10 minutes.
4. Mist the air fryer basket with cooking spray, add the soy curls, and grease them with a bit of cooking spray. Air fry them for 8 to 10 minutes while shaking the basket 2 to 3 times during cooking until they are golden brown and quite crispy.
5. Plate the BBQ soy curls and serve warm.

# BEAN BURGERS WITH VEGAN GARLIC MAYONNAISE

*Servings: 4*

**TOTAL CALORIES:1177**
Protein: 24.56g | Fats: 74.65g | Carbs: 105.47 g

## INGREDIENTS

For the bean patties:
- 675g (cups) black beans cooked and drained
- ¼ diced red onion
- 5g (1 tsp) minced garlic
- 5g (1 tsp) onion powder
- 5g (1 tsp) garlic powder
- 225g (1 cup) panko breadcrumbs
- Salt and black pepper to taste

For the vegan garlic mayonnaise:
- 250ml (1 cup) olive oil
- 10ml (2 tsp) fresh lemon juice
- (125 ml) ½ cup unsweetened soy milk, at room temperature
- 2 garlic cloves, finely minced
- 1g (¼ tsp) salt or to taste

To assemble:
- 4 vegan burger buns, split and toasted
- 4 lettuce leaves
- 4 sliced tomatoes
- Bean patties
- Vegan garlic mayonnaise

## INSTRUCTIONS

For the bean patties:
1. Add the beans to a bowl and coarsely mash with a fork. Add the onion, garlic, onion powder, garlic powder, breadcrumbs, salt, and black pepper. Mix well and form four patties from the mixture.
2. Set the air fryer to 200°C (400°F) for 10 minutes.
3. Grease the air fryer basket with cooking spray, put in the bean patties in a single layer, and mist their tops with cooking spray. Bake for 8 to 10 minutes or until they are golden brown and compact.
4. Transfer them to a plate for assembling.

For the vegan garlic mayonnaise:
5. In a bowl, add the olive oil, lemon juice, soy milk, garlic, and salt. Using a stick or immersion blender, blend the ingredients until smooth and creamy.

To assemble the burgers:
6. On the bottom parts of each burger buns, add one lettuce leaf, top with one tomato slice, one bean patty, and spread on some vegan garlic mayonnaise.
7. Cover with the top buns and serve.

## BLACK BEANS & CORN STUFFE MUSHROOMS

*Servings: 4*

**TOTAL CALORIES: 873**
Protein: 38.43g | Fats: 40.64g | Carbs: 114.02 g

### INGREDIENTS

- 4 large portabella mushrooms, stems and gills removed
- 60ml (4 tbsp) butter, melted
- 15ml (1 tbsp) olive oil
- 1 small yellow onion, finely chopped
- 225g (1 cup) finely-diced bell pepper, any colour of choice
- 5 garlic cloves, minced
- 1 (425g / 15 oz) can black beans, rinsed and drained
- 1 (425g /15 oz) can corn kernels, rinsed
- Salt and black pepper to taste
- 3g (½ tsp) dried oregano
- 3g (½ tsp)) chilli powder, to taste
- 170g (¾ cup) grated vegan cheddar cheese
- Chopped fresh coriander for garnish

### INSTRUCTIONS

1. Rinse the mushrooms well and pat them completely dry with paper towels. After, drizzle the butter on them and set them aside.
2. Heat the olive oil in a skillet over medium heat and sauté the onion and bell pepper for 3 to 4 minutes or until tender. Add the garlic and cook for 1 minute or until fragrant. Stir in the black beans, corn, salt, black pepper, oregano, and chilli powder. Warm through for 3 to 5 minutes.
3. Spoon the corn mixture into the mushrooms and top with the vegan cheddar cheese.
4. Set the air fryer to 190°C (380°F) for 10 minutes.
5. Put the mushrooms in the air fryer basket and bake for 8 to 10 minutes or until the mushrooms are tender and vegan cheese melted.
6. Remove the mushrooms onto serving plates, garnish with coriander, and serve warm.

## BRUSSELS SPROUTS GRATIN

*Servings: 4*

**TOTAL CALORIES: 179**
Protein: 11.59g | Fats: 7.95g | Carbs: 18.12g

### INGREDIENTS

- 450g (16 oz) Brussels sprouts
- Salt and black pepper to taste
- 8g (½ tbsp) butter
- 75g (1/3 cup) chopped shallots
- 10g (2 tsp) all-purpose flour or gluten-free flour
- 170g (¾ cup) fat free milk
- 5g (1 tsp) fresh thyme
- 15g (1 tbsp) grated Parmesan cheese
- 60g (2 oz) grated Gruyere cheese, divided

### INSTRUCTIONS

1. Remove the outer leaves of the Brussels sprouts and cut them in halves. Season them with salt and black pepper, and spread them in a baking dish that can fit into your air fryer.
2. Melt the butter in a skillet and sauté the shallots for 2 minutes. Stir in the flour until it turns light brown. Whisk in the milk and thyme until smooth. Add the Parmesan cheese and half of the Gruyere cheese and mix until melted. Season with salt and black pepper. Pour the sauce over the Brussels sprouts and spread the remaining Gruyere cheese on top.
3. Set the air fryer to 190°C (380°F) for 15 minutes.
4. Place the baking dish in the air fryer and bake for 13 to 15 minutes or until golden brown, the cheese melted, and the sauce is bubbly.
5. Transfer the dish to a heat proof surface and serve warm.

## CHEESY MUSH-ROOM WRAPS

*Servings: 4*

**TOTAL CALORIES: 175**
Protein: 6.85g | Fats: 11.59g |
Carbs: 12.25g

### INGREDIENTS

- 15ml (1 tbsp) olive oil
- 225g (1 cup) sliced white button mushrooms
- Salt and black pepper to taste
- 2 (25cm / 10 inch) whole wheat tortillas
- 15ml (1 tbsp) English mustard
- 43g (1½ oz) Swiss cheese, shredded
- ¼ dill pickle, cubed
- 15ml (1 tbsp) butter, melted

### INSTRUCTIONS

1. Heat the olive oil in a skillet and sauté the mushrooms for 10 to 15 minutes or until its liquid has evaporated and they are golden brown. Season with salt and black pepper.
2. Lay out the tortillas and spread the mustard on top. Add the mushrooms, Swiss cheese, and dill pickle. Wrap up the tortillas and brush them with butter.
3. Set the air fryer to 190°C (375°F) for 10 minutes.
4. Bake the wraps in the air fryer for 4 to 5 minutes per side or until they are golden brown.
5. Take them out onto a plate and slice in halves. Serve warm.

## CHILLI CAULIFLOWER

*Servings: 4*

**TOTAL CALORIES: 48**
Protein: 1.35g | Fats: 3.61g |
Carbs: 3.54g

### INGREDIENTS

- 1 head cauliflower, cut into large florets
- 15ml (1 tbsp) olive oil
- 60ml (¼ cup) hot sauce
- Salt and black pepper to taste

### INSTRUCTIONS

1. Mix the hot sauce, olive oil, salt, and black pepper in a bowl. Add the cauliflower and toss until well-coated.
2. Set the air fryer to 200°C (400°F) for 15 minutes.
3. Add the cauliflower to the air fryer basket and cook for 15 minutes while shaking the basket every 3 minutes or until they are golden brown and tender.
4. Put the cauliflower in a bowl and serve warm.

# CHOPPED SALAD WITH BBQ CHICKPEAS

*Servings: 4*

## TOTAL CALORIES: 428
Protein: 19.33g | Fats: 15.95g | Carbs: 60.68g

## INGREDIENTS

For the BBQ chickpeas:
- 2 (425g / 15 oz) cans chickpeas, drained and rinsed
- 30ml (2 tsp) olive oil
- 5g (1 tsp) paprika
- 5g (1 tsp) maple syrup
- 10g (2 tsp) garlic powder
- 5g (1 tsp) black pepper
- 5g (1 tsp) ground mustard
- 5g (1 tsp) BBQ seasoning

For the chopped salad:
- 45ml (3 tbsp) tahini
- 1 garlic clove, minced
- 30ml (2 tbsp) fresh lemon juice
- 15 to 30g (1 to 2 tbsp) finely-chopped fresh tarragon

Salt to taste
- 2 romaine hearts, chopped
- 110g (½ cup) thinly sliced red onion
- 450g (2 cups) cherry tomatoes, halved
- 1 medium cucumber, peeled and cut into bite-size pieces
- 75g (1/3 cup) pitted kalamata olives, chopped

## INSTRUCTIONS

For the BBQ chickpeas:
1. Pat fry the chickpeas with paper towels and add them to a bowl. In another bowl, mix the olive oil and seasonings until smooth. Add this to the chickpeas and mix well until they are well-coated.
2. Set the air fryer to 190°C (375°F) for 12 minutes.
3. Add the chickpeas to the air fryer basket and roast for 12 minutes while shaking the basket once or twice through cooking until they are golden brown and crispy.
4. Pour them onto a tray and spread them out to cool slightly.

For the salad:
5. In a bowl, whisk the tahini, garlic, lemon juice, tarragon, and salt. Set the dressing aside.
6. In a salad bowl, combine the romaine hearts, onion, tomatoes, cucumber, and olives. Drizzle on the dressing to your taste and toss well.
7. Top with the BBQ chickpeas and serve.

# CORN PUDDING

*Servings: 4*

**TOTAL CALORIES:693**
Protein: 15.11g | Fats: 50.48g
| Carbs: 52.99g

## INGREDIENTS

- 150g (2/3 cup) double cream
- 30ml (2 tbsp) honey
- 120ml (½ cup) salted butter, melted and cooled
- 30g (2 tbsp) granulated sugar
- 2 large eggs, at room temperature, cracked into a bowl
- 420g (14.75 oz) creamed sweet corn
- 430g (15.25 oz) whole corn kernels, drained
- 110g (½ cup) grated cheddar cheese

## INSTRUCTIONS

1. In a bowl, mix the double cream, honey, butter, sugar, and eggs until smooth. Add the creamed sweet corn and whole corn kernels and mix well.
2. Spread the mixture into a baking dish (good for your air fryer) and top with the cheddar cheese.
3. Set the air fryer to 160°C (320°F) for 40 minutes.
4. Bake the pudding for 35 to 40 minutes or until it is golden brown and the sauce is bubbly.
5. Put the baking dish on a heat proof surface and serve warm.

# CRISPY TOFU AND VEGGIE STIR-FRY

*Servings: 4*

**TOTAL CALORIES:223**
Protein: 15.08g | Fats: 8.06g |
Carbs: 25.02g

## INGREDIENTS

- 450g (1 lb) extra firm tofu, pressed and cut into 3cm cubes
- 90ml (6 tbsp soy sauce), low-sodium, divided
- 5ml (1 tsp) toasted sesame oil
- 30g (2 tbsp) corn starch
- Cooking spray
- 1 medium onion, cut into thin wedges
- 1 large red bell pepper, deseeded and cut into chunks
- 1 cup fresh sugar snap pea pods, trimmed
- 45ml (3 tbsp) rice vinegar
- 30ml (2 tbsp) maple syrup
- ¼ tsp red pepper flakes
- 1 tbsp grated fresh ginger

## INSTRUCTIONS

1. In a bowl, toss the tofu with 2 tbsp of soy sauce, sesame oil, and corn starch until well-coated.
2. Set the air fryer to 200°C (400°F) for 15 minutes.
3. Add the tofu to the air fryer basket and air fry for 10 minutes while shaking the basket every 2 to 3 minutes or until they are golden brown and crispy.
4. Mist the onion, bell pepper, and sugar snap pea pods with cooking spray and add them to the air fryer basket. Shake the basket and cook for 5 more minutes or until they are crisp-tender.
5. Meanwhile, as they cook, in a saucepan mix the remaining soy sauce, rice vinegar, maple syrup, red pepper flakes, and ginger. Bring to a boil on a stove top; reduce the heat to low and simmer for 5 minutes or until the sauce has thickened and reduced to half a cup.
6. Add the crispy tofu and veggies to a bowl and drizzle some of the sauce on top to taste. Mix well and serve.

# CRUMBED ASPARAGUS WITH RICOTTA DIP

*Servings: 4*

**TOTAL CALORIES: 365**
Protein: 17.24g | Fats: 16.05g |
Carbs: 38.97g

## INGREDIENTS

For the crumbed asparagus:
- 16 asparagus
- 1 egg
- 15ml (1 tbsp) milk
- 15g (1 tbsp) all-purpose flour or all-purpose flour / gluten-free flour
- 225g (1 cup) panko bread crumbs
- 3g (½ tsp) garlic powder
- 1g (¼ tsp) paprika
- 30g (⅛ cup) grated Parmesan cheese
- Salt and black pepper to taste
- Cooking spray

For the ricotta dip:
- 225g (1 cup) whole milk ricotta cheese
- 3g (½ tsp) honey
- 15ml (1 tbsp) extra virgin olive oil, plus extra for topping
- 20g (1½ tbsp) chopped fresh thyme or oregano
- 1 small garlic clove, minced
- Salt and black pepper to taste
- Fresh chopped thyme for garnish

## INSTRUCTIONS

For the crumbed asparagus:
1. Snap off the hard ends of the asparagus, wash them, and pat them dry.
2. Crack the egg into a bowl and whisk with the milk. On a plate, mix the bread crumbs, garlic powder, paprika, Parmesan cheese, salt, and black pepper.
3. Dip each asparagus in the eggs and coat well with the breadcrumb mixture until well coated. You can repeat the breading process a second time for extra crunch.
4. Set the air fryer to 190°C (380°F) for 16 minutes.
5. Mist the air fryer basket with cooking spray, lay the asparagus in it in a single layer, and mist again with cooking spray.
6. Bake the asparagus for 7 to 8 minutes per side or until they are golden brown.
7. Transfer them to a plate and serve them with the ricotta dip.

For the ricotta dip:
8. In a bowl, add all the ingredients and use a hand mixer to whip until smooth and creamy.
9. Drizzle some olive oil on top, garnish with thyme, and serve with the crumbed asparagus.

## GREEN BEANS, ON-ION, & MUSHROOM CASSEROLE

*Servings: 4*

**TOTAL CALORIES: 187**
Protein: 7.66g | Fats: 8.93g | Carbs: 21.91g

### INGREDIENTS

- 450g (1 lb) fresh green beans, trimmed and cut into thirds
- 400g (14 oz) can cream of mushroom soup
- 15ml (1 tbsp) Worcestershire sauce
- 120ml (½ cup) almond milk
- 3g (½ tsp) garlic powder
- Salt and black pepper to taste
- 225g (1 cup) fried onions
- 60g (¼ cup) cheese, optional

### INSTRUCTIONS

1. Add the green beans to a baking dish and mist with cooking spray.
2. Set the air fryer to 170°C (340°F) for 12 minutes.
3. Place the dish in the air fryer and bake for 12 minutes, stirring them every 3 minutes or until tender.
4. Meanwhile, in a bowl, mix the cream of mushroom soup, Worcestershire sauce, almond milk, garlic powder, salt, and black pepper.
5. Take out the green beans when ready and spread the creamed soup mixture on top. Spread on the fried onions and Parmesan cheese if using.
6. Bake the dish further in the air fryer at 170°C (340°F) for 1 to 2 minutes.
7. Remove the dish and serve warm.

## HERBED SPRING ROLLS

*Servings: 4*

**TOTAL CALORIES: 141**
Protein: 5.45g | Fats: 0.8g | Carbs: 28.35g

### INGREDIENTS

- 1 cup cabbage slaw mix
- 2 salad onions, chopped
- 1 small red bell pepper, deseeded and chopped
- 15g (1 tbsp) chopped fresh parsley
- 3g (½ tsp) red pepper flakes
- 5ml (1 tsp) soy sauce, low-sodium
- 1 large egg white
- 5ml (1 tsp) water
- 5g (1 tsp) corn starch
- 4 (17cm / 6.5 inch) egg roll wrappers each

### INSTRUCTIONS

1. In a bowl, mix the cabbage slaw mix, salad onions, red bell pepper, parsley, red pepper flakes, and soy sauce. In a bowl, beat the egg white, corn starch, and water until smooth.
2. Lay out each egg roll wrapper and spoon the vegetable mixture at the centre, about ¼ cup for each. Brush the edges of the wrappers with the egg mixture and roll up the wrappers over the filling by folding over the sides and then rolling the opposite sides from one end until it seals.
3. Set the air fryer to 200°C (400°F) for 10 minutes.
4. Grease the air fryer basket with cooking spray, lay in the spring rolls, and grease them with cooking spray. Air fry for 4 to 5 minutes per side or until they are golden brown and crispy.
5. Transfer them to a paper towel-lined plate to drain grease and serve warm.

## HERBED TOFU

*Servings: 4*

### TOTAL CALORIES: 112
Protein: 11.19g | Fats: 7.14g | Carbs: 2.98g

### INGREDIENTS

- 450g (1 lb) block of extra firm tofu, pressed
- 3ml (½ tsp) olive oil
- 5g (1 tsp) dried mixed herb seasoning
- Salt and black pepper to taste
- Chopped fresh coriander for garnish

### INSTRUCTIONS

1. Cut the tofu into 2cm cubes and add them to a bowl. In another bowl, mix the olive oil, mixed herb seasoning, salt, and black pepper. Pour the seasoning over the tofu and toss until well-coated.
2. Set the air fryer to 200°C (400°F) for 10 minutes.
3. Add the tofu to the air fryer basket and air fry for 10 minutes while shaking the basket every 2 to 3 minutes or until they are golden brown all around.
4. Remove the tofu into a bowl, garnish with coriander, and serve warm.

## JUNIPER CAULIFLOWER STEAKS

*Servings: 4*

### TOTAL CALORIES: 118
Protein: 1.64g | Fats: 10.64g | Carbs: 5.68g

### INGREDIENTS

- 1 large head cauliflower
- 45ml (3 tbsp) olive oil
- 2 tsp minced garlic
- 3g (½ tsp) ground juniper berries
- 3g (½ tsp) salt or to taste
- 3g (½ tsp) black pepper to taste
- 15g (1 tbsp) chopped parsley
- Lemon wedges for serving

### INSTRUCTIONS

1. Stand the cauliflower and using a sharp knife, cut 4 to 6 steak shapes by slicing from top to bottom.
2. In a bowl, mix the olive oil, garlic, juniper berries, salt, and black pepper. Brush the seasoning on both sides of the cauliflower steaks.
3. Set the air fryer to 160°C (380°F) for 15 minutes.
4. Lay the cauliflower steaks in the air fryer basket and bake for 12 to 15 minutes or until they are golden brown and tender.
5. Plate the cauliflower steaks, garnish with parsley, and serve with lemon wedges.

# MUSHROOM AND RICE CASSEROLE

*Servings: 4*

**TOTAL CALORIES: 874**
Protein: 20.65g | Fats: 57.16g | | Carbs: 74.22g

## INGREDIENTS

- 30g (2 tbsp) butter
- 450g (1 lb) sliced fresh mushrooms
- 1 medium onion, chopped
- Salt and black pepper to taste
- 280g (1¼) cups uncooked rice
- 110g (½ cup) sliced almonds
- 720ml (3 cups) chicken broth
- 360ml (1½ cups) double cream
- 45g (3 tbsp) grated Old Winchester cheese

## INSTRUCTIONS

1. Melt the butter in a pot and sauté the mushrooms for 10 minutes or until most of its liquid has evaporated. Add the onion and sauté for 3 minutes or until tender. Season with salt and black pepper, and stir in the rice, almonds, and double cream.
2. Pour the rice mixture onto a baking dish and cover with foil.
3. Set the air fryer to 175°C (350°F) for 75 minutes.
4. Bake the dish in the air fryer for 65 to 70 minutes or until the rice is tender. Remove the foil and spread the cheese on top. Bake further for 5 minutes or until the cheese melts.
5. Take out the dish, let cool for 5 to 10 minutes, and serve warm.

---

# PAPRIKA TOFU

*Servings: 4*

**TOTAL CALORIES: 128**
Protein: 11.76g | Fats: 7.32g | Carbs: 8.81g

## INGREDIENTS

- 450g (1 lb) block of extra firm tofu, pressed
- 3g (½ tsp) onion powder
- 5g (1 tsp) garlic powder
- 5g (1 tsp) paprika
- 10g (2 tsp) corn starch
- 8ml (½ tbsp) light soy sauce, low sodium
- 3ml (½ tsp) sesame oil
- Salt and black pepper to taste

## INSTRUCTIONS

1. Cut the tofu into 2cm cubes and add them to a bowl. In another bowl, mix the onion powder, garlic powder, paprika, corn starch, soy sauce, sesame oil, salt, and black pepper. Pour the seasoning over the tofu and toss until well-coated.
2. Set the air fryer to 200°C (400°F) for 10 minutes.
3. Add the tofu to the air fryer basket and air fry for 10 minutes while shaking the basket every 2 to 3 minutes or until they are golden brown all around.
4. Remove the tofu into a bowl and serve.

# PEAS AND TOMATO FILO PACKETS

Servings: 4

**TOTAL CALORIES: 822**
Protein: 5.66g | Fats: 76g |
Carbs: 33.09g

## INGREDIENTS

- 15ml (1 tbsp) olive oil
- 2 salad onions, finely chopped
- 1 garlic clove, minced
- 110g (½ cup) cherry tomatoes, quartered
- 15g (1 tbsp) chopped fresh dill
- 110g (½ cup) frozen garden peas, defrosted
- Salt and black pepper to taste
- 4 sheets filo pastry, cut into 20 equal squares
- 20 butcher's string for tying
- Olive oil for brushing

## INSTRUCTIONS

1. Heat the olive oil in a skillet and sauté the salad onions and garlic for 1 minute. Toss in the tomatoes, dill, and peas. Season with salt and black pepper, and let warm for 2 minutes. Turn the heat off.
2. Divide the peas mixture into 20 equal portions and add each to the centre of each filo pastry. Grab the four corners of one pastry and hold them together over the filling. Carefully twist or use butcher's strings to tie it into a parcel. Repeat the same process with the other pastries and brush them with olive oil.
3. Set the air fryer to 180°C (360°F) for 15 minutes.
4. Place the pastry parcels in the air fryer basket and bake for 12 to 15 minutes or until they are golden brown and warm through.
5. Transfer them to a platter and serve them warm.

# QUINOA AND CORN STUFFED PEPPERS

Servings: 4

**TOTAL CALORIES: 343**
Protein: 9.24g | Fats: 20.81g |
Carbs: 33g

## INGREDIENTS

- 2 large bell peppers, any colour of choice
- 90ml (4 tbsp) butter, melted
- Salt and black pepper to taste
- 15ml (1 tbsp) olive oil
- 1 small yellow onion, finely chopped
- 1 small green bell pepper, deseeded and diced
- 5 garlic cloves, minced
- 225g (1 cup) cooked quinoa
- 1 (425g / 15oz) can sweet corn kernels, drained
- 3g (½ tsp) dried parsley
- 3g (½ tsp) chilli powder, to taste
- 60g (¾ cup) shredded vegan mozzarella cheese
- Chopped fresh coriander for garnish

## INSTRUCTIONS

1. Cut the peppers in halves lengthwise and remove their seeds and membranes. Drizzle them with the butter and season them with salt and black pepper.
2. Heat the olive oil in a skillet over medium heat and sauté the onion and bell pepper for 3 to 4 minutes or until tender. Stir in the garlic and cook for 1 minute or until fragrant. Stir in the quinoa, corn, parsley, chilli powder, salt, black pepper. Turn the heat off.
3. Spoon the quinoa mixture into the peppers and top with the vegan mozzarella cheese.
4. Set the air fryer to 190°C (380°F) for 10 minutes.
5. Put the peppers in the air fryer basket with the cheese side facing upwards and bake for 8 to 10 minutes or until the peppers are tender and vegan mozzarella melted.
6. Plate the peppers, garnish with coriander, and serve warm.

## SOFT CHEESE PASTA DISH

*Servings: 4*

**TOTAL CALORIES: 301**
Protein: 11.25g | Fats: 19.62g | | Carbs: 20.52g

### INGREDIENTS

- 170g (6 oz) rigatoni or other pasta of choice
- 15ml (1 tbsp) olive oil
- 1 medium white onion, diced
- 1 red bell pepper, deseeded and diced
- Salt and black pepper to taste
- 240ml (1 cup) pasta sauce
- 60g (¼ cup) soft cheese
- 110g (½ cup) grated cheddar cheese

### INSTRUCTIONS

1. Cook the pasta according to the package's instructions until al dente. Drain and add the pasta to a bowl. Set aside.
2. Heat the olive oil in a pot and sauté the onion and bell pepper for 5 minutes or until tender. Turn the heat off.
3. Add the pasta, pasta sauce, salt, black pepper, and soft cheese. Mix until well-combined and spread the mixture in a baking dish (with good size for your air fryer). Spread the cheddar cheese on top.
4. Set the air fryer to 180°C (360°F) for 9 minutes.
5. Place the dish in the air fryer and bake for 7 to 9 minutes or until the cheeses melt and the top is golden brown.
6. Remove the dish, let rest for 5 minutes, and serve warm.

## SWEET PEPPER PIZZAS WITH RICOTTA

*Servings: 4*

**TOTAL CALORIES: 465**
Protein: 24.8g | Fats: 27.95g | Carbs: 29.5g

### INGREDIENTS

- 4 (10cm / 4 inch) flatbreads
- 15ml (1 tbsp) olive oil
- 1 to 2 garlic cloves, minced
- 225g (1 cup) ricotta cheese
- 2 sweet peppers, different colours, deseeded and thinly sliced
- 225g (1 cup) shredded mozzarella cheese
- Fresh basil leaves for topping

### INSTRUCTIONS

1. On each flatbread, brush some olive oil and spread the garlic on top. Spread the ricotta cheese on top, followed by the sweet peppers, and mozzarella cheese.
2. Set the air fryer to 200°C (400°F) for 15 minutes.
3. One after the other, bake each pizza in the air fryer for 12 to 15 minutes or until the cheese melts and the peppers are tender.
4. Take them out, top with fresh basil, drizzle on some olive oil, and serve warm.

# SWEET POTATO AND LENTILS ROLLS

(IN MINUTES)
PREP
**15**
COOK
**12**

*Servings: 4*

**TOTAL CALORIES: 1379**
Protein: 43.63g | Fats: 75.29g | Carbs: 136.51g

## INGREDIENTS

For the filling:
- 2 tbsp olive oil
- 1 red onion, finely diced
- 1 garlic clove, minced
- 45g (3 tsp) all-purpose vegetable seasoning
- 400g (1 lb) sweet potato, cooked and mashed
- 200g (1 cup) lentils, cooked
- 110g (½ cup) rolled oats
- 110g (½ cup) breadcrumbs

- 165g (1½ cups) vegan cheddar cheese
- 30g (2 tbsp) chopped fresh parsley
- Salt and black pepper to taste

For the pastry:
- 1 pack of filo pastry, about 10 sheets
- 60ml (¼ cup) vegan egg substitute, prepared
- 30g (2 tsp) white or black sesame seeds

## INSTRUCTIONS

For the filling:
1. Heat the olive oil in a skillet and sauté the onion for 3 minutes or until tender. Add the garlic and vegetables seasoning; sauté for 30 seconds or until fragrant. Turn the heat off and stir in the mashed sweet potatoes, lentils, oats, breadcrumbs, parsley, salt, and black pepper.

For the pastry:
2. Double the filo pastry sheets and lay them out. Divide the filling into five parts and add one portion to each pastry. Wrap the pastry over the filling, with a little water on your finger, dab their edges, and seal them. Turn over the pastries and brush them with the vegan egg substitute and sprinkle the sesame seeds on top.
3. Set the air fryer to 200°C (400°F) for 12 minutes.
4. Grease the air fryer basket with cooking spray and place the rolls in it. Bake them for 10 to 12 minutes or until they are golden brown.
5. Remove them onto a wire rack, let them cool slightly, and serve.

*How about some lunch meals that can be done in the air fryer all together. That's what this set is about, with options like meatball rolls, pizza pockets, and others that would get you full lunches in a little time. You may not need side dishes in most cases.*

DON'T FORGET TO GET THE

**TOP RECIPES** FROM THIS BOOK
AS

**A FREE DOWNLOADABLE PDF IN COLOUR**

**SCAN THE QR CODE BELOW**

*Just follow the steps below to access it via the QR Code (the picture code at the bottom of this page) or click the link if you are reading this on your Phone / Device.*

1. Unlock your phone & open up the phone's camera
2. Make sure you are using the "back" camera (as if you were taking a photo of someone) and point it towards the QR code at the bottom of the page.
3. Tap your phone's screen exactly where the QR code is.
4. A link / pop up will appear. Simply tap that (and make sure you have internet connection) and the FREE PDF containing all of the colored images should appear.

# BAKED POTATO SALAD

 **1**

*Servings: 4*

**TOTAL CALORIES: 864**
Protein: 26.55g | Fats: 61.76g | Carbs: 53.83g

## INGREDIENTS

- 900g (2 lb) russet potatoes
- 240ml (1 cup) soured cream
- 240ml (1 cup) mayonnaise
- 5 salad onions, chopped
- 8 bacon slices, cooked and chopped
- 225g (1 cup) shredded cheddar cheese
- Salt and black pepper to taste

## INSTRUCTIONS

1. Wash the potatoes well and use a fork to prick them all around.
2. Set the air fryer to 200°C (400°F) for 40 minutes.
3. Place the potatoes in the air fryer and bake for 30 to 40 minutes or until they tender.
4. Take them out and let them cool completely. Peel them after and cut them into rough cubes.
5. Add the potatoes to a bowl and mix in the soured cream, mayonnaise, salad onions, bacon, cheddar cheese, salt, and black pepper.

---

# BBQ PORK BURGERS

 **2**

*Servings: 4*

**TOTAL CALORIES: 554**
Protein: 24.42g | Fats: 26.13g | Carbs: 53.42g |

## INGREDIENTS

For the burger patties:
- 450g (1 lb) pork mince
- 10g (2 tsp) BBQ seasoning
- Salt and black pepper to taste

To assemble the burgers:
- 4 hamburger buns, split and toasted
- 4 lettuce leaves
- 4 sliced tomatoes
- 4 red onion slices
- BBQ sauce for topping

## INSTRUCTIONS

For the pork patties:
1. Mix the pork, BBQ seasoning, salt, and black pepper in a bowl and form 4 equal patties from it.
2. Set the air fryer to 200°C (400°F) for 12 minutes.
3. Grease the air fryer basket with cooking spray, lay the pork patties in it, and mist their tops with cooking spray. Bake for 10 to 12 minutes or until they are golden brown and cooked through.
4. Put the patties on a plate and let them rest for 10 minutes.

To assemble the burgers:
5. On the bottom parts of each burger buns, add one lettuce leaf, top with one tomato slice, one pork patty, one red onion slice, and some BBQ sauce.
6. Cover with the top buns and serve.

## BEEF, OLIVES, & MUSHROOM HAND PIES

*Servings: 4*

(IN MINUTES)
PREP **10**
COOK **10**

**TOTAL CALORIES: 711**
Protein: 30.1g | Fats: 46.39g | | Carbs: 44.73g

### iNGREDiENTS

- 15ml (1 tbsp) olive oil
- 450g (1 lb) beef mince
- 110g (½ cup) chopped white button mushrooms
- 2 garlic cloves, minced
- 1 tsp ground cumin
- 5g (1 tsp) chilli powder
- Salt and black pepper to taste
- 110g (½ cup) pitted olives, chopped
- 2 refrigerated pie crusts
- 1 large egg
- 1 tbsp water

### iNSTRUCTiONS

1. Heat olive oil in the skillet and cook the beef mince for 5 minutes or until it is starting to get brown. Add the mushrooms and cook until most of the liquid has evaporated. Stir in the garlic, cook for 1 minute and season with cumin, chilli powder, salt, and black pepper.
2. Lay out the pie crusts on a flat surface and cut out 4 (10cm / 4-inch diameter) circles from them.
3. Divide the beef mixture into four parts and add a portion to the centre of each pie crust. Fold the crust over the filling and use a fork to crimp their edges to seal.
4. Crack the egg into a bowl and whisk with the water. Brush the tops of the pastry with the egg wash.
5. Set the air fryer to 175°C (350°F) for 10 minutes.
6. Grease the air fryer basket with cooking spray, place the pastries in it in a single layer, and bake for 8 to 10 minutes or until they are golden brown.
7. Remove the hand pies onto a wire rack and let cool slightly before serving.

---

## BRIE AND POTATO HAND PIES

*Servings: 4*

(IN MINUTES)
PREP **10**
COOK **10**

**TOTAL CALORIES: 675**
Protein: 22.18g | Fats: 48.38g | Carbs: 38.46g

### iNGREDiENTS

- 300g (2/3 lb) potatoes, cut into ½-inch cubes and cooked
- 1 bacon slice, cooked and chopped
- 120ml (½ cup) double cream
- 120ml (½ cup) milk
- 1 garlic clove, crushed
- 15ml (3 tsp) wholegrain mustard
- 125g (9 oz) double brie, finely chopped
- 4 sheets frozen puff pastry, just thawed
- 1 salad onion, finely chopped
- 1 egg, lightly whisked
- 5g (1 tsp) poppy seeds
- 5g (1 tsp) sesame seeds

### iNSTRUCTiONS

1. In a bowl, mix the potatoes, bacon, double cream, milk, garlic, mustard, and brie.
2. Lay out the pie crusts on a flat surface and cut out 4 (10cm / 4-inch diameter) circles from them.
3. Add 60g / ¼ cup of the potato brie mixture onto the centre of each pie crust. Top with the salad onion. Fold the crust over the filling and use a fork to crimp their edges to seal.
4. Brush their tops with the egg and sprinkle the sesame seeds and poppy seeds on top.
5. Set the air fryer to 175°C (350°F) for 10 minutes.
6. Grease the air fryer basket with cooking spray, place the pastries in it in a single layer, and bake for 8 to 10 minutes or until they are golden brown.
7. Remove the hand pies onto a wire rack and let cool slightly before serving.

*THE UK AIR FRYER COOKBOOK*

# BROCCOLI AND SHRIMP

(IN MINUTES)
PREP 10
COOK 8

*Servings: 4*

## TOTAL CALORIES: 250
Protein: 31.39g | Fats: 8.7g | Carbs: 14.13g

## INGREDIENTS

- 1 head broccoli, separated into small florets
- 450g (1 lb) jumbo shrimp, peeled and deveined
- 15ml (1 tbsp) olive oil
- 15ml (1 tbsp) minced garlic
- 15ml (1 tbsp) mixed herb seasoning
- Salt and black pepper to taste
- 60g (¼ cup) grated Parmesan cheese

## INSTRUCTIONS

1. Add all the ingredients to a bowl and mix well.
2. Set the air fryer to 200°C (390°F) for 8 minutes.
3. Add the broccoli and shrimp mix into the air fryer basket and cook for 6 to 8 minutes while shaking the basket every 2 to 3 minutes during cooking or until the shrimp is opaque and the broccoli is crisp-tender to your desire.
4. Plate the broccoli and shrimp and serve warm.

# CASHEW CHICKEN STIR-FRY

(IN MINUTES)
PREP 20
COOK 12

*Servings: 4*

## TOTAL CALORIES: 428
Protein: 26.62g | Fats: 26.8g | Carbs: 20.75g

## INGREDIENTS

For the marinade:
- 60ml (¼ cup) hoisin sauce
- 1 tbsp white vinegar
- 60ml (¼ cup) soy sauce, low sodium
- 15g (1 tbsp) white sugar
- 30g (2 tbsp) grated fresh ginger
- 5g (1 tsp) corn starch
- 450g (1 lb) chicken thighs, boneless and skinless

For the stir-fry:
- 5g (1 tsp) olive oil
- 30g (2 tbsp) minced garlic
- 1 carrot, cut into thick slices
- 30g (2 tbsp) salad onions, chopped
- 75g (1/3 cup) roasted cashew halves

## INSTRUCTIONS

For the marinade:
1. Combine the marinade ingredients in a bowl (except for the chicken) and mix well. Add the chicken, toss well, and cover the bowl with cling film. Refrigerate for 30 minutes.

For the stir-fry:
2. Set the air fryer to 190°C (380°F) for 12 minutes.
3. Remove the chicken from the fridge and using tongs, pick them into another bowl. Add the olive oil, garlic, carrot, and salad onions. Toss well.
4. Add the chicken mixture to the air fryer basket and cook for 10 to 12 minutes while stirring 2 to 3 times during cooking.
5. Add the cashews after 10 minutes of cooking and let them warm through.
6. Serve the stir-fry with rice.

# CHEESY CORN CRUNCHWRAPS

*Servings: 4*

**TOTAL CALORIES: 1010**
Protein: 42.23g | Fats: 63.85g
| Carbs: 68.26g

## INGREDIENTS

- 450g (2 cups) shredded cooked chicken
- 450g (2 cups) canned sweetcorn, drained
- 450g (2 cups) shredded mozzarella cheese
- 10g (2 tsp) dried oregano
- 15g (1 tbsp) chopped fresh coriander
- Salt to taste
- 1g (¼ tsp) red chilli flakes
- 4 large tortilla wraps
- Guacamole for serving

## INSTRUCTIONS

1. Add the chicken, sweetcorn, mozzarella, oregano, salt, and red chilli flakes to a bowl and mix.
2. Divide the mixture into four parts and add a portion to the centre of each tortilla. Fold the sides of the tortilla over the filling and roll over from the opposite end until covered.
3. Set the air fryer to 190°C (380°F) for 6 minutes.
4. Grease the air fryer basket with cooking spray, put the wraps in it and toast for 2 to 3 minutes per side or until they are golden brown and well-warmed.
5. Transfer them to a chopping board and slice them in halves. Serve the crunchwraps warm with guacamole.

# CHICKEN PIE POCKETS

*Servings: 4*

**TOTAL CALORIES: 240**
Protein: 11.11g | Fats: 15.52g |
Carbs: 13.4g

## INGREDIENTS

- 2 (300g / 10.5 oz) cans cream of chicken soup
- 1 tsp garlic powder
- 1 (300g / 10 oz bag) frozen vegetables (carrot, green beans, and corn mix)
- 1 small roasted chicken, meat shredded and the bones discarded
- Salt and black pepper to taste
- 2 refrigerated pie crusts
- 1 large egg, beaten

## INSTRUCTIONS

1. In a bowl, mix the cream of chicken soup, garlic powder, vegetables, chicken, salt, and black pepper.
2. Lay the pie crusts on a flat surface and cut out 4 (10cm / 4-inch diameter) circles from them.
3. Add 60g (¼ cup) of the chicken mixture to their centres, fold the crust over the filling, and pinch their edges to seal. Brush them with the egg.
4. Set the air fryer to 175°C (350°F) for 25 minutes.
5. Grease the air fryer basket with cooking spray, place the pastries in it in a single layer, and bake for 20 to 25 minutes or until they are golden brown and warmed within.
6. Plate them, let them cool slightly, and serve after.

## CHICKEN AND RICE STUFFED PEPPERS

*Servings: 4*

**TOTAL CALORIES: 284**
Protein: 11.78g | Fats: 17.98g | Carbs: 18.62g

### INGREDIENTS

- 4 large bell peppers
- 15ml (1 tsp) olive oil for drizzling
- Salt and black pepper to taste
- 110g (½ cup) chopped or shredded cooked chicken
- 110g (½ cup) cooked brown or white rice
- 110g (½ cup) shredded cheddar cheese, divided
- 3 salad onions, finely chopped, plus extra for garnish
- 3g (½ tsp) mixed herb seasoning
- 1 to 3g (¼ to ½ tsp) red pepper flakes
- 3g (½ tsp) garlic powder

### INSTRUCTIONS

1. Cut the peppers in halves lengthwise and clean out the seeds and membranes. Drizzle them with a little olive oil, season with salt and black pepper, and set them aside.
2. In a bowl, add the remaining ingredients (but leave half of the cheddar cheese for topping) and mix well. Spoon the mixture into the peppers and top with the remaining cheddar cheese.
3. Set the peppers in the air fryer and bake for 6 to 8 minutes or until they are tender.
4. Transfer the peppers to a plate, garnish with some salad onions, and serve warm.

## CLASSIC CHEESEBURGERS

*Servings: 4*

**TOTAL CALORIES: 440**
Protein: 31.37g | Fats: 29.54g | Carbs: 13.18g

### INGREDIENTS

- 450g (1 lb) beef mince
- 15ml (1 tbsp) soy sauce, low sodium
- 2 garlic cloves, minced
- Salt and black pepper to taste
- 4 slices cheddar cheese

To assemble:
- 4 hamburger buns, split and toasted
- Thinly sliced red onions
- Sliced tomatoes
- Mayonnaise

### INSTRUCTIONS

For the beef patties:
1. In a bowl, mix the beef mince, soy sauce, garlic, salt, and black pepper. Form four equal patties from the mixture.
2. Set the air fryer to 200°C (400°F) for 12 minutes.
3. Grease the air fryer basket with cooking spray, lay in the beef patties, and mist their tops with cooking spray. Bake for 10 minutes or until they are golden brown and cooked through.
4. Lay one cheese slice on each patty and bake for 2 more minutes or until the cheese melts over the patties.

To assemble the burgers:
5. On the bottom parts of each burger bun, add some onion slices, one cheeseburger patty, tomatoes, and mayonnaise.
6. Cover with the top buns and serve.

# MEATBALL ROLLS

*Servings: 4*

**TOTAL CALORIES: 854**
Protein: 42.77g | Fats: 43.11g | | Carbs: 73.87g

## INGREDIENTS

For the meatballs:
- 450g (1 lb) beef mince
- 1 egg, cracked into a bowl
- 15ml (1 tbsp) Worcestershire sauce
- 60g (¼ cup) breadcrumbs
- 60g (¼ cup) grated Old Winchester or Parmesan cheese
- 5g (1 tsp) garlic powder
- Salt and black pepper to taste

To assemble:
- 480ml (2 cups) pasta sauce
- 4 hot dog buns, split lengthwise
- 225g (1 cup) grated mozzarella cheese

## INSTRUCTIONS

For the meatballs:
1. In a bowl, mix the beef mince, egg, Worcestershire sauce, breadcrumbs, cheese, salt, and black pepper. Form 16 meatballs from the mixture.
2. Set the air fryer to 190°C (380°F) for 14 minutes.
3. Grease the air fryer with cooking spray, arrange the meatballs in it in a single layer, and mist their tops with cooking spray. Cook for 12 to 14 minutes or until they are golden brown and cooked within. Turn the meatballs halfway through cooking.
4. Take them out when ready and let them rest for 5 minutes.

To assemble:
5. Spread the pasta sauce inside both sides of the hot dog buns and add four meatballs in each.
6. Place them in the air fryer with the opened side facing upwards and spread the mozzarella cheese on top.
7. Bake at 190°C (380°F) for 2 to 3 minutes or until the cheese melts.
8. Take them out and serve them warm.

# PEPPERS AND HERB TOASTIES

*Servings: 4*

**TOTAL CALORIES: 169**
Protein: 6.26g | Fats: 13.25g | Carbs: 6.65g

## INGREDIENTS

- 2 slices bread
- 5 to 10g (1 to 2 tsp) butter, at room temperature
- 2 or 3 slices cheddar cheese
- 110g (½ cup) chopped mixed bell peppers
- 15g (1 tbsp) each chopped fresh parsley and thyme

## INSTRUCTIONS

1. Spread the butter on both sides of the bread. Lay them down and load one piece with 1 cheese slice, the bell peppers and herbs, top with the remaining cheese, and cover with the other bread slice.
2. Set the air fryer to 185°C (370°F) for 5 minutes.
3. Put the bread in the air fryer basket and toast for 3 to 5 minutes or until the cheese melts.
4. Take it out, slice in halves and serve.

## PINEAPPLE TOFU RICE BOWLS

(IN MINUTES)
PREP 10
COOK 40

*Servings: 4*

### TOTAL CALORIES: 412
Protein: 17.25g | Fats: 23.25g | Carbs: 40.25g

### INGREDIENTS

For the pineapple tofu:
- 450g (1 lb) firm tofu, pressed
- 225g (1 cup) chopped pineapple
- 5ml (1 tsp) olive oil
- 60ml (¼ cup) sweet soy sauce
- 60ml (¼ cup) hot sauce or to taste
- 3 stalks scallions, chopped

For the rice bowls:
- 225 to 450g (1 to 2 cups) cooked white rice
- 2 avocados, peeled, pitted, and sliced
- Pickled carrots
- 2 green onions, sliced
- Sesame seeds for garnish

### INSTRUCTIONS

For the pineapple tofu:
1. Cut the tofu into 2.5cm (1-inch cubes) and add it to a bowl. Add the pineapple, olive oil, soy sauce, hot sauce, and scallions. Mix well.
2. Set the air fryer to 200°C (400°F) for 40 minutes.
3. Spoon the tofu and pineapple into the air fryer basket and bake for 30 to 40 minutes or until the tofu is golden brown while stirring every 10 minutes.
4. Remove the pineapple tofu onto a plate when ready.

For the rice bowls:
5. Divide the rice into 4 bowls and top with the avocados, carrots, pineapple tofu, green onions, and sesame seeds.
6. Serve the rice bowls.

## SHRIMP, TOMATO, & ONION MIX

(IN MINUTES)
PREP 10
COOK 5

*Servings: 4*

### TOTAL CALORIES: 127
Protein: 23.56g | Fats: 1.6g | Carbs: 3.29g

### INGREDIENTS
- 450g (1 lb) shrimp, peeled and deveined
- Salt and black pepper to taste
- 1 small onion, thinly sliced
- 110g (½ cup) cherry tomatoes
- 1 lime, juiced

### INSTRUCTIONS

1. Season the shrimp and add it to a bowl. Add the tomatoes, onion, butter, and lime juice. Toss well.
2. Set the air fryer to 175°C (350°F) for 8 minutes.
3. Add the shrimp mixture to the air fryer basket and cook for 6 to 8 minutes or until the shrimp is opaque.
4. Dish the shrimp and tomato mix and serve warm.

## SPICY STEAK LETTUCE WRAPS

*Servings: 4*

**TOTAL CALORIES: 320**
Protein: 25.23g | Fats: 19.76g
| Carbs: 9.5g

### INGREDIENTS

- 450g (1 lb) boneless beef top sirloin steak, cut into thin strips
- 15ml (1 tbsp) soy sauce, low sodium
- 30ml (2 tbsp) chilli garlic sauce
- 15ml (1 tbsp) olive oil
- 5g (1 tsp) grated fresh ginger
- 1g (¼ tsp) salt or to taste
- 110g (½ cup) match-stick cut carrots
- 110g (½ cup) thinly sliced yellow onion
- 110g (½ cup) match-stick cut red bell pepper
- 12 small romaine lettuce leaves
- 110g (½ cup) match-stick cut cucumber
- Lime wedges, optional

### INSTRUCTIONS

1. In a bowl, combine the beef, soy sauce, chilli garlic sauce, olive oil, ginger, salt, carrots, yellow onion, and red bell pepper.
2. Set the air fryer to 200°C (400°F) for 12 minutes.
3. Add the beef and veggies to the air fryer and cook for 10 to 12 minutes or until the beef cooks through and the vegetables are tender.
4. Arrange the lettuce leaves on a platter and spoon the beef and veggie mix into them. Top with the cucumber and serve warm with lime wedges.

## SPINACH SEA BASS PACKS

*Servings: 4*

**TOTAL CALORIES: 352**
Protein: 43.46g | Fats: 16.71g
| Carbs: 2.51g

### INGREDIENTS

- 22.5g (1½ tbsp) melted butter for brushing
- 60ml (4 tbsp) cold unsalted butter, cut into small pieces
- 1 (142g / 5 oz) bag baby spinach
- 4 (226g / 8 oz) skinless sea bass fillets
- Salt and black pepper to taste
- 1 medium shallot, minced
- 60ml (¼ cup) dry white wine

### INSTRUCTIONS

1. Cut out 4 large aluminium foil pieces and lay them out. Brush their tops with butter.
2. Top each one with the spinach, one sea bass fillet each, and season with salt and black pepper. Add the shallot, dry white wine, and the butter cubes. Wrap up the foil over the fish.
3. Set the air fryer to 200°C (400°F) for 10 minutes.
4. Bake the fish in the air fryer for 8 to 10 minutes.
5. Transfer the packs to a plate, let cool slightly and serve warm.

*THE UK AIR FRYER COOKBOOK*

## STEAK & MUSH-ROOM BITES

*Servings: 4*

**TOTAL CALORIES: 359**
Protein: 22.05g | Fats: 29.54g
| Carbs: 2.47g

## SWEET ONION TARTS

*Servings: 4*

**TOTAL CALORIES: 290**
Protein: 6.25g | Fats: 23.13g |
Carbs: 15g

### INGREDIENTS

- 450g (1 lb) rib eye steak, cut into bite-size cubes
- 225g (8 oz) white button mushrooms, cleaned and sliced
- 30ml (2 tbsp) melted butter
- 5 ml (1 tsp) Worcestershire sauce
- 2.5 g (½ tsp) garlic powder
- Salt and black pepper to taste
- Minced fresh parsley for garnish
- Red pepper flakes for garnish

### INSTRUCTIONS

1. In a bowl, toss the steak, mushrooms, butter, Worcestershire sauce, garlic, salt, and black pepper.
2. Set the air fryer to 200°C (400°F) for 8 minutes.
3. Add the steak and mushrooms to the air fryer and cook for 6 to 8 minutes or until the mushrooms are tender and the steak cooked through.
4. Plate the broccoli and shrimp and serve warm.

### INGREDIENTS

- 2 sheets shortcrust pastry, just defrosted
- 15ml (1 tbsp) olive oil
- 2 small brown onions, thinly sliced
- 75g (¾ cup) soft cheese
- 30ml (2 tbsp) soured cream
- 25g (¼ cup) grated cheddar
- 1 egg, cracked into a bowl
- Chopped fresh chives for garnish
- You'll need some baking beans

### INSTRUCTIONS

1. Grease 4 small tart pans with cooking spray and set them aside.
2. Roll out each pastry into 3mm thickness and cut them into four pieces. Line each tart pan with one pastry, line them with parchment paper and spread some baking beans on them.
3. Set the air fryer to 200°C (400°F) for 8 minutes.
4. Bake the pastry in the air fryer for 6 minutes. Pour out the baking beans and remove the parchment paper. Bake further for 2 minutes and remove them.
5. Meanwhile, heat the olive oil in a skillet over low heat and sauté the onion for 10 to 15 minutes or until they are caramelised.
6. Spoon the onions into a bowl and add the soft cheese, soured cream, cheddar cheese, and egg. Spoon and spread the mixture in the tart cases.
7. Place the tart in the air fryer and bake for 170°C (340°F) for 10 to 12 minutes or until they are golden brown.
8. Take out the tarts, let them cool slightly and serve.

## THREE CHEESE PIZZA POCKETS

*Servings: 4*

**TOTAL CALORIES: 638**
Protein: 31g | Fats: 30.38g |
Carbs: 60.47g

### INGREDIENTS

- 1 (462g / 16.3 oz) can refrigerated biscuits, 8 pieces
- 60ml (¼ cup) marinara or pizza sauce
- 110g (½ cup) shredded mozzarella cheese
- 110g (½ cup) grated Parmesan cheese
- 110g (½ cup) shredded Gruyere cheese
- 15g (1 tbsp) chopped fresh basil
- 1 large egg
- 15ml (1 tbsp) water

### INSTRUCTIONS

1. Separate the biscuits into 16 pieces and flatten them with your hands.
2. Spread the pizza sauce on 8 of the biscuits. Mix the cheeses in a bowl, divide them onto the biscuits, and top with the basil. Cover with the other 8 biscuits and fold their ends over each other to seal.
3. Crack the egg into a bowl and whisk with the water. Brush the egg wash on the pastry.
4. Set the air fryer to 175°C (350°F) for 10 minutes.
5. Grease the air fryer basket with cooking spray, place the biscuits in it without overlapping, and bake for 8 to 10 minutes or until they are golden brown.
6. Remove the hand pies onto a wire rack, let them cool slightly, and serve.

## TOFU MANGO STIR-FRY

*Servings: 4*

**TOTAL CALORIES: 198**
Protein: 14.97g | Fats: 7.21g |
Carbs: 23.52g

### INGREDIENTS

- 80ml (1/3 cup) soy sauce, low sodium
- 15ml (1 tbsp) rice vinegar
- 30g (2 tbsp) coconut sugar
- 5g (1 tsp) garlic powder
- 1g (¼ tsp) ground ginger
- 450g (1 lb) extra firm tofu, pressed and cut into bite-size pieces
- 1 each red and green bell pepper, de-seeded and cut into chunks
- 1 small mango, peeled and diced
- Sliced green onion, for garnish

### INSTRUCTIONS

1. In a bowl, mix the soy sauce, rice vinegar, coconut sugar, garlic powder, and ground ginger until smooth. Add the tofu and bell peppers. Mix well.
2. Set the air fryer to 190°C (380°F) for 10 minutes.
3. Add the tofu pepper mix to the air fryer basket and cook for 6 to 8 minutes or until the tofu is light golden. Stir in the mango and cook for 2 minutes.
4. Plate the stir-fry, garnish with the green onion, and serve warm.

# TOMATO AND CHEESE TARTS

(IN MINUTES)
PREP
**10**
COOK
**30**

*Servings: 4*

## TOTAL CALORIES: 343
Protein: 12.56g | Fats: 22.5g | Carbs: 21.72g

## INGREDIENTS

- 2 sheets shortcrust pastry, just defrosted
- 15ml (1 tbsp) olive oil
- 2 large onions, thinly sliced
- 3 large garlic cloves, sliced
- Salt and black pepper to taste
- 45ml (3 tbsp) dry white wine
- 10g (2 tsp) minced fresh thyme leaves

- 60g (4 tbsp) grated Parmesan cheese, plus extra for topping
- 110g (4 oz) soft goat cheese
- 1 large tomato, cut into ¼-inch slices
- 45g (3 tbsp) basil chiffonade

## INSTRUCTIONS

1. Grease four small tart pans with cooking spray and set them aside.
2. Roll out each pastry into 3mm thickness and cut them into four pieces. Line each tart pan with one pastry, line them with parchment paper and spread some baking beans on them.
3. Set air fryer to 200°C (400°F) for 8 minutes.
4. Bake pastry in air fryer for 6 minutes. Pour out baking beans and remove parchment paper. Bake further for 2 minutes and remove them.
5. Meanwhile, heat the olive oil in a skillet over low heat and sauté onions for 10 minutes or until they are very tender. Add garlic and cook for 1 minute or until fragrant. Season with salt and black pepper. Pour in white wine, add thyme. Cook until wine has reduced by half. Turn heat off and stir in parmesan cheese and goat cheese.
6. Spoon onion-cheese mixture in the tart cases and top with the tomato slices and then some more parmesan cheese and basil.
7. Place the tart in the air fryer and bake for 170°C (340°F) for 10 to 12 minutes or until they are golden brown and the cheese has melted.

# TURKEY MELT ROLLS

*Servings: 4*

**TOTAL CALORIES: 479**
Protein: 28.2g | Fats: 20.22g |
Carbs: 46.37g

## INGREDIENTS

- 15ml (1 tbsp) melted butter
- 3g (½ tsp) garlic salt
- 12 dinner rolls, split
- 340g (12 oz) sliced deli turkey
- 6 slices mozzarella cheese, each divide to make 12 pieces

## INSTRUCTIONS

1. Brush the inner sides of the dinner rolls with butter and season with garlic salt. Lay one deli turkey and one mozzarella slice in each. Close the buns and brush their tops with butter.
2. Set the air fryer to 175°C (350°F) for 10 minutes.
3. Put the rolls in the air fryer basket and bake for 8 to 10 minutes or until the cheeses melt.
4. Take them out and serve them warm.

# TURKEY AND VEGGIE MIX

*Servings: 4*

**TOTAL CALORIES: 288**
Protein: 26.74g | Fats: 15.02g |
Carbs: 10.4g

## INGREDIENTS

- 450g (1 lb) turkey breasts, cut into bite-size pieces
- 225g (1 cup) broccoli florets
- 1 courgette, chopped
- 225g (1 cup) diced bell peppers, mixed colours
- ½ white onion, cut into chunks
- 2 garlic cloves, minced
- 30ml (2 tbsp) olive oil
- 15g (1 tbsp) mixed herb seasoning
- 3g (½ tsp) each chilli powder and garlic powder
- Salt and black pepper to taste

## INSTRUCTIONS

1. Add all the ingredients to a bowl and mix well.
2. Set the air fryer to 190°C (380°F) for 12 minutes.
3. Pour the turkey and veggie mix into the air fryer basket and cook for 10 to 12 minutes while stirring every 3 to 4 minutes or until the chicken cooks through and the veggies are crisp tender.
4. Spoon the turkey and veggie mix into a bowl and serve with rice or other grains.

*Fixing up a hefty dinner after a long day out isn't often the best feeling. Finding ways to make a quick and easy dinner time that is healthy, tasty, and filling is the way out. With the air fryer, you can organise dinner in such little time while you unpack for the day. Here are some ideas to check out.*

DON'T FORGET TO GET THE

**TOP RECIPES** FROM THIS BOOK
AS

**A FREE DOWNLOADABLE PDF IN COLOUR**

**SCAN THE QR CODE BELOW**

*Just follow the steps below to access it via the QR Code (the picture code at the bottom of this page) or click the link if you are reading this on your Phone / Device.*

1. Unlock your phone & open up the phone's camera
2. Make sure you are using the "back" camera (as if you were taking a photo of someone) and point it towards the QR code at the bottom of the page.
3. Tap your phone's screen exactly where the QR code is.
4. A link / pop up will appear. Simply tap that (and make sure you have internet connection) and the FREE PDF containing all of the colored images should appear.

# BACON, CHICKEN, & CREAM ROLL UPS

*Servings: 4*

## TOTAL CALORIES: 869
Protein: 78.54g | Fats: 59.38g | Carbs: 1.91g

### INGREDIENTS

- 4 chicken breasts, boneless skinless
- 8 bacon slices
- 227g (8 oz) soft cheese, at room temperature
- 113g (4 oz) frozen spinach, thawed and well drained
- 5g (1 tsp) fresh lemon zest
- 5g (1 tsp) fresh lemon juice
- Salt and black pepper to taste
- Toothpicks to secure

### INSTRUCTIONS

1. Wrap each chicken in cling film and gently lb with a rolling pin until flattened.
2. Lay the 2 bacon slices closely to each other and repeat with the other 6 slices. Place one chicken on each bacon set.
3. In a bowl, mix the soft cheese, spinach, lemon zest, lime zest, salt, and black pepper. Mix well and spread the mixture on the chicken.
4. Roll the bacon and chicken over the filling and secure the ends with toothpicks.
5. Set the air fryer to 190°C (375°F) for 25 minutes.
6. Bake the chicken roll ups in the air fryer for 20 to 25 minutes or until the bacon is golden brown and the chicken reaches an internal temperature of 83°C (165°F)

# BAKED BEANS CASSEROLE

*Servings: 4*

## TOTAL CALORIES: 487
Protein: 20.24g | Fats: 18.8g | Carbs: 70.26g

### INGREDIENTS

- 4 bacon slices, chopped
- 225g (1 cup) chopped yellow onion
- 15ml (1 tbsp) dill pickle juice
- 180ml (¾ cup) barbecue sauce
- 30ml (2 tbsp) Worcestershire sauce
- 120ml (½ cup) ketchup
- 30ml (2 tbsp) yellow mustard
- 5g (1 tsp) smoked paprika
- 5g (1 tsp) garlic powder
- 2 (425g / 15 oz) cans navy beans, rinsed and drained

### INSTRUCTIONS

1. Cook the bacon in a skillet over medium heat for 10 minutes or until golden brown and crispy. Remove the bacon onto a plate and set it aside.
2. Sauté the onion in the same skillet and cook for 3 minutes. Stir in the pickle juice, barbecue sauce, Worcestershire sauce, ketchup, mustard, paprika, and garlic powder. Let come to a boil and stir in the navy beans.
3. Transfer the mixture to a baking dish that can fit into your air fryer, sprinkle the bacon on top, and cover with foil.
4. Set the air fryer to 180°C (360°F) for 20 minutes.
5. Bake for 15 to 20 minutes or until the beans warm through and the sauce thickens.
6. Take out the dish, remove the foil, and serve warm.

## BAKED SWEET POTATOES & CHOPPED PORK

*Servings: 4*

### TOTAL CALORIES: 509
Protein: 23.17g | Fats: 30.38g | Carbs: 38.24g

## INGREDIENTS

- 75g (1/3 lb) shredded pork roast
- 20ml (1 and1/3 tbsp) butter, melted
- 150g (2/3 cup) peeled and diced apples
- 150g (2/3 cups) diced onion
- 5ml (1 tsp) apple cider vinegar
- 2g (1/3 tsp) ground cinnamon
- 10g (2 tsp) minced fresh ginger
- Salt and black pepper to taste
- 4 medium sweet potatoes, precooked
- 75g (1/3 cup) diced bacon
- 225g (1 cup) grated cheddar cheese
- Chopped fresh cilantro for garnish

## INSTRUCTIONS

1. In a bowl, mix the pork roast, butter, apples, onion, apple cider vinegar, cinnamon, ginger, salt, and black pepper.
2. Burst the sweet potatoes open to create boats and spoon the pork mixture into them. Top with the bacon and cheddar cheese.
3. Place the sweet potatoes in the air fryer and bake for 15 to 20 minutes or until the cheese melts.
4. Transfer the sweet potatoes to a platter and serve warm.

## BEEF QUINOA BAKE

*Servings: 4*

### TOTAL CALORIES: 806
Protein: 45.57g | Fats: 39.94g | Carbs: 71.58g

## INGREDIENTS

- 225g (1 cup) cooked quinoa
- 225g (1 cup) cooked beef mince
- 1 (440g / 15.5 oz) can black beans, drained and rinsed
- 1 green chilli pepper, chopped
- 1 sweet onion, diced
- 225g (1 cup) frozen corn kernels
- 10g (2 tsp) chilli powder
- 5g (1 tsp) ground cumin
- 240ml (1 cup) chicken broth
- 240ml (1 cup) salsa
- 225g (1 cup) grated cheddar cheese

For serving:

- Chopped salad onions
- Soured cream
- Chopped fresh parsley

## INSTRUCTIONS

1. Mix all the casserole's ingredients in a bowl except for the cheese. Spread the mixture in a baking dish that's a good size for your air fryer and spread the cheddar cheese on top.
2. Set the air fryer to 190°C (350°F) for 20 minutes.
3. Bake the dish in the air fryer for 15 to 20 minutes or until the cheese melts and is golden brown.
4. Take out the dish, top with some salad onions, soured cream, and parsley, and serve warm.

# BEEF AND BROCCOLI

*Servings: 4*

## TOTAL CALORIES: 273
Protein: 29.46g | Fats: 5.73g | Carbs: 27.78g

## INGREDIENTS

For the beef and broccoli:
- 450g (1 lb) sirloin tip steak, thinly sliced
- 15ml (1 tbsp) soy sauce
- 5g (1 tsp) onion powder
- 5g (1 tsp) garlic powder
- 30g (2 tbsp) corn starch
- 340g (12 oz) broccoli florets, cut into bite-sized pieces
- Cooking spray

For the sauce:
- 80ml (1/3 cup) light soy sauce
- 7ml (1½ tsp) rice vinegar
- 30g (2 tbsp) light brown sugar, packed
- 45ml (3 tbsp) beef stock
- 4 garlic clove, minced
- 5g (1 tsp) minced fresh ginger
- 15g (1 tbsp) corn starch

## INSTRUCTIONS

For the beef and broccoli:
1. Toss the steak with the soy sauce, onion powder, garlic powder, and corn starch. Set it aside.
2. Set the air fryer to 170°C (340°F) for 8 minutes.
3. Add the broccoli to the air fryer, mist with cooking spray, and cook for 6 to 8 minutes while shaking the basket every 2 minutes. When the broccoli is tender, transfer it to a plate.
4. Add the steak to the air fryer, mist with cooking spray, and cook at the same temperature for 15 minutes or until the beef is brown and cooked.

For the sauce:
5. Meanwhile, in a saucepan, mix the soy sauce, rice vinegar, light brown sugar, beef stock, garlic, ginger, and corn starch until smooth. Cook over low heat until the sauce thickens.
6. Add the beef to the broccoli when ready, toss in the sauce, and serve.

## BURRITO-STUFFED CHICKEN

*Servings: 4*

### TOTAL CALORIES: 866
Protein: 74.74g | Fats: 35.85g | Carbs: 57.86g

### INGREDIENTS

- 4 chicken breasts, skinless and boneless
- Salt and black pepper to taste
- 80ml (1/3 cup) hot sauce
- 170g (¾ cup) cooked rice
- 125g (4.4 oz) can black beans, drained and rinsed
- 1 green shallot, thinly sliced
- 80g (1 cup) shredded mozzarella
- Toothpicks for securing
- 170g (6 oz) packet cheese supreme corn chips, toasted
- 2 eggs
- 60g (¼ cup) plain flour
- Avocado dip for serving

### INSTRUCTIONS

1. Butterfly the chicken and season with salt and black pepper.
2. Spread the hot sauce on one side of each chicken breast and then top with the rice, black beans, green shallot, and mozzarella. Wrap the empty side of the chicken over the filling and secure the ends with toothpicks.
3. Crush the corn chips in a food processor until fine. Crack the eggs into a bowl and beat lightly. Add the flour to a plate.
4. Coat the stuffed chicken in the flour, then in the eggs, and dress well with the corn chips.
5. Set the air fryer to 180°C (360°F) for 12 minutes.
6. Grease the air fryer basket with cooking spray, add the chicken without overlapping, and mist again with cooking spray.
7. Fry the chicken for 5 to 6 minutes per side or until golden brown and the chicken reaches an internal temperature of 74°C (165°F).
8. Plate the chicken and let them rest for 5 minutes before serving.

## CAULIFLOWER AND SAUSAGE CASSEROLE

*Servings: 4*

### TOTAL CALORIES: 359
Protein: 20.55g | Fats: 27.76g | Carbs: 7.59g

### INGREDIENTS

- 15ml (1 tbsp) olive oil
- 340g (12 oz) cauliflower, cut into bite-sized pieces
- Salt and black pepper to taste
- 225g (1 cup) sliced sausages
- 5g (1 tsp) dried oregano
- 1 cup shredded Gruyere cheese

### INSTRUCTIONS

1. In a baking dish (good for your air fryer), mix the cauliflower, salt, black pepper, sausage, and oregano. Spread the cheese on top.
2. Set the air fryer to 190°C (380°F) for 10 minutes.
3. Bake the cauliflower and sausage for 8 to 10 minutes or until the cauliflower is tender.
4. Dish the food and serve warm.

# COCONUT CRUMBED PORK WITH PINEAPPLE SALAD

*Servings: 4*

**TOTAL CALORIES: 1172**
Protein: 51.53g | Fats: 63.73g | Carbs: 103.11g

## INGREDIENTS

For the coconut-crumbed pork:
- 4 pork chops, boneless
- Salt and black pepper to taste
- 110g (½ cup) all-purpose flour / gluten-free flour
- 2 eggs, lightly beaten
- 450g (2 cups) finely shredded coconut flakes

For the pineapple salad:
- 1 pineapple, cut into chunks
- 1 red onion, thinly sliced
- 1 red bell pepper, deseeded and diced

- 1 cucumber, deseeded and cut into half-moon shapes
- 1 avocado, pitted and diced
- 1 jalapeno, deseeded and diced
- 60g (¼ cup) chopped fresh cilantro

For the salad dressing:
- 60ml (¼ cup) olive oil
- 30ml (2 tbsp) lime juice
- 30ml (2 tbsp) honey
- 5ml (1 tsp) white vinegar
- 3g (½ tsp) red pepper flakes, crushed
- Salt and black pepper to taste

## INSTRUCTIONS

For the coconut-crusted pork chops:
1. Pat the pork chops dry with paper towels and season them with salt and black pepper.
2. Dredge the pork in the flour, dip in the eggs, and then coat well with the shredded coconut.
3. Set the air fryer to 200°C (400°F) for 12 minutes.
4. Mist the air fryer basket with cooking spray, add the pork chops, mist them again with cooking spray, and bake them for 10 to 12 minutes or until the pork chops are golden brown and reach an internal temperature of 62°C (145°F).
5. Remove them onto a plate and let them rest for 10 minutes while you make the salad.

For the pineapple salad:
6. Add all the ingredients to a bowl and mix well.

For the salad dressing:
7. Whisk all the ingredients in a bowl and pour over the salad. Mix well.
8. Serve the pork chops with the pineapple salad.

# FISH TACOS & WITH CHILLI LIME SAUCE

*Servings: 4*

**TOTAL CALORIES: 501**
Protein: 24.76g | Fats: 15.77g | Carbs: 66.91g

## INGREDIENTS

For the fish:
- 2 white fish fillets, cut into 3cm (1-inch) cubes
- Salt and black pepper to taste
- 5g (1 tsp) spicy paprika
- 5g (1 tsp) ground cumin
- 3g (½ tsp) chilli flakes
- 15ml (1 tbsp) olive oil
- 30ml (2 tbsp) fresh lime juice

For the tacos:
- 8 small tortillas
- ¼ small red cabbage, shredded
- 2 small baby gem lettuces, shredded
- 1 large ripe mango, peeled and diced
- Fresh cilantro leaves
- Sliced pickled jalapenos
- 200ml (2/3 cup) soured cream
- Lime wedges

## INSTRUCTIONS

1. For the fish:
2. In a bowl, add the fish ingredients and mix well.
3. Set the air fryer to 175°C (350°F) for 15 minutes.
4. Cook the fish in the air fryer for 10 to 15 minutes or until they are golden brown and flaky.
5. Remove them onto a plate.
6. For the tacos:
7. Add the fish to the tortillas and top with the cabbage, lettuce, mango, cilantro, jalapenos, and soured cream.
8. Serve the tacos with the lime wedges.

# FRIED GOAT CHEESE & ROCKET SALAD

*Servings: 4*

(IN MINUTES)
PREP
10
COOK
6

**TOTAL CALORIES: 351**
Protein: 20.28g | Fats: 15.79g | Carbs: 35.29g

## INGREDIENTS

For the fried goat cheese:
- 1 (110g / 4 oz) log of goat cheese, frozen
- 60g (¼ cup) flour
- 1 egg, beaten
- 110g (½ cup) seasoned bread crumbs
- Cooking spray

For the salad:
- 450g (2 cups) baby rocket
- 450g (2 cups) baby spinach
- ¼ small red onion, thinly sliced
- 15 to 30g (1 to 2 tbsp) dried cranberries, to taste
- 15 to 30g (1 to 2 tbsp) candied pecans to taste
- Fresh black pepper to taste

## INSTRUCTIONS

1. For the fried goat cheese:
2. Cut the goat cheese into 4 to 6 coins.
3. Dredge the goat cheese in the flour, then dip in the eggs, and coat well in the breadcrumbs. Dip it in the egg again and then coat well with breadcrumbs. Place the goat cheese in the fridge for 20 minutes to firm up again.
4. Set the air fryer to 175°C (350°F) for 6 minutes.
5. Grease the air fryer basket with cooking spray and fry the breaded goat cheese for 1 to 3 minutes per side or until golden brown and crispy.
6. For the salad:
7. In a bowl, combine the rocket, spinach, red onion, cranberries, candied pecans, and black pepper. Mix well and top with the fried goat cheese.

## HADDOCK & CAU-LIFLOWER FOIL PACKS

*Servings: 4*

**TOTAL CALORIES: 318**
Protein: 33.8g | Fats: 16.87g | Carbs: 8.33g

### INGREDIENTS

- 4 haddock fillets, cut into 3cm (1-inch) pieces
- 1 cauliflower head, cut into florets
- 15ml (1 tbsp) olive oil
- Salt and black pepper to taste
- 5 garlic cloves, grated
- 15g (1½ tsp) dried oregano
- 15g (1 tbsp) fresh thyme leaves
- 3g (½ tsp) red pepper flakes
- 60g (4 tbsp) cold butter
- 15g (1 tbsp) chopped fresh parsley for garnish

### INSTRUCTIONS

1. Cut out four large foil papers and lay them out separately.
2. Divide the haddock and cauliflower on top. Drizzle with olive oil and season with salt and black pepper. Add the garlic, oregano, thyme, red pepper flakes, and butter.
3. Set the air fryer to 200°C (400°F) for 10 minutes.
4. Place the foil packs in the air fryer and bake for 10 minutes or until the shrimp is flaky and the cauliflower is tender.
5. Remove the foil packs onto serving plates, let cool slightly and serve.

## LEMON PRAWNS AND VEGGIE FOIL PACKETS

*Servings: 4*

**TOTAL CALORIES: 350**
Protein: 37.53g | Fats: 19.45g | Carbs: 9.28g

### INGREDIENTS

- 675g (1½ lb) prawns, peeled and deveined
- 450g (1 lb) asparagus, cut into thirds
- 1 red bell pepper, deseeded and cut into strips
- 1 yellow bell pepper, deseeded and cut into strips

For the lemon garlic butter sauce:
- 90g (6 tbsp) salted butter, at room temperature
- 30ml (2 tbsp) fresh lemon juice
- 8 garlic cloves, minced
- Salt and black pepper to taste
- 30g (2 tbsp) chopped fresh parsley
- 3g (½ tsp) red pepper flakes

### INSTRUCTIONS

1. Cut out four large foil papers and lay them out separately.
2. Divide the prawns, asparagus, and bell peppers onto them.
3. In a bowl, mix the butter, lemon juice, garlic, parsley, red pepper flakes, salt, and black pepper. Spoon the butter over the mixture and wrap the foil over the prawns and veggies.
4. Set the air fryer to 200°C (400°F) for 10 minutes.
5. Place the foil packs in the air fryer and bake for 8 to 10 minutes or until the shrimp is opaque and the veggies are tender.
6. Remove the foil packs onto serving plates, let cool slightly and serve.

## LOADED BAKED SPAGHETTI SQUASH

*Servings: 4*

**TOTAL CALORIES:601**
Protein: 48.49g | Fats: 28.89g
| Carbs: 42.66g

### INGREDIENTS

- 1.35kg (3 lb) spaghetti squash
- 450g (1 lb) beef mince
- Salt and black pepper to taste
- 1 small onion, diced
- 2 garlic cloves, minced
- 710ml (24 oz) pasta sauce
- 5g (1 tsp) mixed herb seasoning
- 225g (1 cup) shredded mozzarella cheese, plus extra for topping
- 110g (½ cup) grated Parmesan cheese

### INSTRUCTIONS

1. Cut the butternut squash in halves and scoop the seeds out. Discard them.
2. Set the air fryer to 185°C (370°F) for 30 minutes.
3. Put the squash in the air fryer and bake for 20 to 30 minutes or until the flesh is tender.

Meanwhile, prepare the filling.

4. Heat the olive oil in a skillet and cook the beef mince for 5 minutes. Season with salt, black pepper, and stir in the onion and garlic. Continue cooking for 5 more minutes or until the beef is brown. Stir in the pasta sauce and mixed herb seasoning.
5. Remove the squash when ready and use a fork to shred the flesh into a bowl. Mix the flesh with the mozzarella cheese and then back to the squash casing.
6. Spoon the beef mince on top and spread some more mozzarella cheese and Parmesan cheese on top.
7. Bake for 10 more minutes or until the cheese melts and the filling is bubbly.

## LOADED PASTA BITES

*Servings: 4*

**TOTAL CALORIES: 824**
Protein: 47.79g | Fats: 50.25g |
Carbs: 50.45g

### INGREDIENTS

- 24 jumbo pasta shells, cooked and patted dry
- 60ml (¼ cup) extra virgin olive oil
- 450g (1 lb) beef mince
- 1 small red onion, chopped
- 10g (2 tsp) ground cumin
- 5g (1 tsp) garlic powder
- 10g (2 tsp) ground coriander
- 375ml (13 oz) jar salsa, thick and chunky
- 125g (4.4 oz) can black beans
- 8g (1½ tsp) chilli powder
- 225g (1 cup) grated cheddar
- 2 tomatoes, diced
- 1 avocado, diced
- Chopped fresh coriander for garnish
- Soured cream for serving
- Lime wedges for serving

### INSTRUCTIONS

1. Arrange the cooked pasta shells on a tray with open sides facing upwards.
2. Heat the olive oil in a skillet and cook the beef mince for 5 minutes. Add the onion and cook for 3 to 5 minutes or until the beef is brown. Season with the cumin, garlic powder, and coriander and cook for 1 minute.
3. Turn the heat off and stir in the salsa, chilli powder, black beans, and two-third of the cheese. Spoon the mixture into the pasta shells and top with the remaining cheese.
4. Set the air fryer to 190°C (375°F) for 8 minutes.
5. Place the pasta shells in the air fryer and bake for 6 to 8 minutes or until they are golden brown and the cheese has melted.
6. Put them on a platter and top them with tomatoes, avocado, and coriander.
7. Serve them with some soured cream and lime wedges.

*THE UK AIR FRYER COOKBOOK*

## OLD WINCHESTER BRUSSELS SPROUTS AND CAULIFLOWER

*Servings: 4*

### TOTAL CALORIES: 526
Protein: 3.69g | Fats: 55.02g |
Carbs: 8.18g

### INGREDIENTS

- 225g (½ lb) Brussels sprouts, trimmed and halved
- 225g (½ lb) cauliflower florets
- 15ml (1 tbsp) extra-virgin olive oil
- Salt and black pepper to taste
- Grated Old Winchester cheese for serving

### INSTRUCTIONS

1. Combine the Brussels sprouts, cauliflower, olive oil, salt, and black pepper. Toss well and add them to the air fryer basket.
2. Set the air fryer to 175°C (350°F) for 15 minutes.
3. Place the baking dish in the air fryer and bake for 13 to 15 minutes or until golden brown and the vegetables are tender.
4. Pour the veggies into a bowl, top with the Old Winchester cheese and serve warm.

## OLIVE AND CHEESE-STUFFED MEATLOAF

*Servings: 4*

### TOTAL CALORIES: 766
Protein: 54.27g | Fats: 48.83g |
Carbs: 29.11g

### INGREDIENTS

- 675g (1½ lb) beef mince
- 120ml (½ cup) milk
- 15ml (1 tbsp) Worcestershire sauce
- 2 large eggs, lightly beaten
- 225g (1 cup) crushed cornflakes
- 45g (3 tbsp) finely chopped celery
- 110g (½ cup) finely chopped onion
- 5g (1 tsp) salt or to taste
- 1g (¼ tsp) black pepper or to taste
- 3g (½ tsp) ground mustard
- 3g (½ tsp) rubbed sage
- 225g (1 cup) cubed cheddar cheese
- 110g (½ cup) sliced pimiento-stuffed olives

### INSTRUCTIONS

1. Line a loaf pan (good for your air fryer) with foil with a bit of it falling over the loaf pan for lifting the meatloaf when ready.
2. Add all the ingredients to a bowl except for the cheddar cheese and olives and mix them well. Fold the cheese cubes and olives into the mixture. Spoon the beef mix into the loaf pan and mould to fit the shape of the loaf pan.
3. Set the air fryer to 175°C (350°F) for 20 minutes.
4. Place the loaf pan in the air fryer and bake for 18 to 20 minutes or until the meat is longer pink within.
5. Take out the loaf pan and let the meatloaf rest in it for 10 minutes. Carefully, hold the hanging sides of the foil and lift the meatloaf onto a serving platter.
6. Slice and serve warm.

## PEAS AND CORN FRIED RICE

*Servings: 4*

**TOTAL CALORIES: 370**
Protein: 14.28g | Fats: 12.64g | Carbs: 50.2g

### INGREDIENTS

- 30g (2 tbsp) unsalted butter, melted
- 675g (3 cups) cold cooked rice or left-overs
- 225g (1 cup) scrambled eggs
- 110g (½ cup) canned sweet corn kernels, drained
- 110g (½ cup) garden peas, frozen, not thawed
- ½ cup diced red bell pepper
- 1 small onion, diced
- 3 garlic cloves, minced
- 15ml (1 tbsp) oyster sauce
- 30ml (2 tbsp) soy sauce, low sodium
- 5ml (1 tsp) sesame oil
- Chopped fresh salad onions for garnish

### INSTRUCTIONS

1. In an air fryer safe baking dish, combine the butter, rice, eggs, corn, peas, onion, garlic, oyster sauce, soy sauce, and sesame oil. Mix well.
2. Set the air fryer to 175°C (350°F) for 15 minutes.
3. Place the dish in the air fryer and cook for 10 to 15 minutes or until the rice and vegetables warm through.
4. Dish the fried rice, garnish with salad onions, and serve warm.

## PEPPERONI FLAT-BREAD PIZZA

*Servings: 4*

**TOTAL CALORIES: 482**
Protein: 28.25g | Fats: 32.2g | Carbs: 18.49g

### INGREDIENTS

- 4 flat breads
- 120ml (½ cup) pizza sauce
- 340g (1½ cups) shredded mozzarella cheese
- 110g (½ cup) sliced pepperoni

### INSTRUCTIONS

1. Spread the pizza sauce on the flat breads and top with the mozzarella cheese and pepperoni.
2. Set the air fryer to 200°C (400°F) for 8 minutes.
3. One after the other, bake the pizza in the air fryer for 6 to 8 minutes or until the cheese melts.
4. Slice and serve the ready pizza warm.

# PORK BELLY SKEWERS WITH WARM KALE SALAD

**19**

Servings: 4

(IN MINUTES)
PREP
**10**
COOK
**14**

## TOTAL CALORIES: 994
Protein: 19.96g | Fats: 90.31g | Carbs: 30.13g

## INGREDIENTS

For the pork belly skewers:
- 450g (1 lb) pork belly, cut into bite-size cubes
- 1 small courgette, sliced
- 1 onion, quartered
- 15ml (1 tbsp) olive oil
- 15ml (1 tbsp) soy sauce, low sodium
- 3ml (½ tsp) fish sauce
- 10ml (2 tsp) honey
- 15g (1 tbsp) sweet chilli sauce
- 3g (½ tsp) chilli oil, optional
- Salt and black pepper to taste

For the warm kale salad:
- 1 bunch kale, cut into very thin ribbons
- Salt to taste
- 60ml (¼ cup) extra virgin olive oil
- 4 garlic cloves, minced
- ½ lemon, zested and juiced
- 75g (1/3 cup) golden raisins
- Salt and black pepper to taste
- 75g (1/3 cup) coarsely chopped toasted almonds
- Shaved Parmesan cheese for topping

## INSTRUCTIONS

For the pork belly skewers:

1. On 4 skewers, alternately thread the pork belly, courgettes, and onion. Place them on a plate.
2. In a bowl, mix the olive oil, soy sauce, fish sauce, honey, sweet chilli sauce, chilli oil, salt, and black pepper. Brush the sauce over both sides of the pork skewers.
3. Set the air fryer to 160°C (380°F) for 12 minutes.
4. Cook the skewers in the air fryer for 6 minutes per side or until they are golden brown and the pork reaches an internal temperature of 62°C (145°F). Brush them again with the sauce when you turn them.
5. Remove them onto a plate to rest for 5 to 10 minutes while you make the salad.

For the warm kale salad:
6. Season the kale with some salt in a bowl and press the kale through your fists a few times to help soften them. Set it aside.
7. Heat the olive oil in a skillet and sauté the garlic for 1 minute or until fragrant. Stir in the raisins, salt, and black pepper. Add the kale and toss for 1 minute.
8. Add the kale to a bowl and top with the almonds and Parmesan shavings.
9. Serve the pork belly skewers with the Parmesan shavings.

# PORK, CUCUMBER, & SPINACH WRAPS

*Servings: 4*

(IN MINUTES)
PREP **10**
COOK **20**

## TOTAL CALORIES: 242

Protein: 34g | Fats: 5.42g | Carbs: 14.59g

## INGREDIENTS

For the pork:
- 3 pork chops, boneless
- Salt and black pepper to taste
- 80ml (1/3 cup) soy sauce
- 10ml (2 tsp) Worcestershire sauce
- 30g (2 tbsp) brown sugar
- 5ml (1 tsp) Dijon mustard
- 2 garlic cloves, minced

For the spinach or tortilla wraps:
- 16 large spinach leaves
- 1 English cucumber, halved and thinly sliced
- 1 green chilli pepper, thinly sliced
- 2 salad onions, thinly sliced
- Chopped fresh cilantro to garnish
- Sweet chilli sauce for topping
- 1 lime, sliced into wedges

## INSTRUCTIONS

For the pork:
1. Season the pork with salt and black pepper and place in a zipper bag. In a bowl, mix the soy sauce, Worcestershire sauce, brown sugar, mustard, and garlic. Pour the mixture over the pork chops and massage well. Marinate in the fridge for 20 minutes.
2. Set the air fryer to 200°C (400°F) for 12 minutes.
3. Remove the pork from the marinade and place in the air fryer. Cook for 6 minutes per side or until the pork is golden brown and reaches an internal temperature of 73°C (145°F).
4. Remove the pork from the air fryer and let it rest for 10 minutes.
5. Thinly slice after.

For the spinach wraps:
6. On each spinach, add some pork slices, cucumber, salad onions, cilantro, and sweet chilli sauce.
7. Serve with lime wedges.

# QUINOA & SPINACH STUFFED CHICKEN

*Servings: 4*

(IN MINUTES)
PREP **10**
COOK **10**

## TOTAL CALORIES: 1133

Protein: 109.41g | Fats: 68.36g | Carbs: 17.8g

## INGREDIENTS

- 4 medium chicken breasts, skinless and boneless
- 15ml (1 tbsp) olive oil
- Salt and black pepper to taste
- 225g (1 cup) cooked quinoa
- 450g (2 cups) fresh spinach, chopped
- 170g (6 oz) feta cheese, crumbled
- A pinch of red pepper flakes

## INSTRUCTIONS

1. Butterfly each chicken, rub them with the olive oil and season with salt and black pepper.
2. In a bowl, mix the quinoa, spinach, feta cheese, red pepper flakes, salt, and black pepper. Spoon the mixture on one side of each chicken and fold the empty side over the filling. Seal the ends with toothpicks.
3. Set the air fryer to 175°C (350°F) for 10 minutes.
4. Place the chicken in the air fryer basket and cook for 4 to 5 minutes per side or until the chicken is golden brown and reaches an internal temperature of 74°C (165°F).
5. Plate the chicken, let it rest for 5 minutes, and serve.

## SALMON RICE PATTIES

*Servings: 4*

**TOTAL CALORIES: 433**
Protein: 47.01g | Fats: 19.8g | Carbs: 13.82g

### INGREDIENTS

- 2 salmon fillets, cooked
- 60g (¼ cup) cooked short-grain rice
- 60g (¼ cup) breadcrumbs
- 2 eggs, cracked into a bowl
- 60ml (¼ cup) mayonnaise
- 5ml (1 tsp) hot sauce, optional
- 5g (1 tsp) grated fresh ginger
- 1g (¼ tsp) salt
- 1 lemon, zested
- 3g (½ tsp) dried dill
- Cooking spray

### INSTRUCTIONS

1. Put all the ingredients into a bowl and mix well. Form 4 equal patties from the mixture
2. Set the air fryer to 200°C (390°F) for 8 minutes.
3. Mist the air fryer basket with cooking spray and add the patties to it. You can cook them two at a time. Grease them again and cook for 3 to 4 minutes per side.
4. Put the patties on a plate and serve with your favourite sauce, salads, vegetables, etc.

## TURKEY PASTA BAKE

*Servings: 4*

**TOTAL CALORIES: 1164**
Protein: 82.87g | Fats: 61.38g | Carbs: 68.62g

### INGREDIENTS

- 15ml (1 tbsp) olive oil
- 225g (1 cup) sliced mushrooms
- 1 leek, roughly chopped
- 2 garlic cloves, minced
- 250g (1 lb) dry pasta shells or macaroni
- 240ml (1 cup) turkey or chicken stock
- 300ml (1¼ cups) water
- Salt and black pepper to taste
- 2 big handfuls fresh baby spinach leaves
- 675g (3 cups) cooked turkey, roughly chopped
- 240ml (1 cup) double cream
- 225g (1 cup) shredded Gruyere cheese
- 225g (1 cup) shredded mozzarella cheese

### INSTRUCTIONS

1. Heat the olive oil in a skillet and sauté the mushrooms for 10 to 12 minutes or until the liquid has evaporated and they are turning golden brown. Stir in the leek and cook for 5 minutes or until tender. Add the garlic and cook for 1 minute or until fragrant.
2. Stir in the pasta, turkey or chicken stock, water, and season with salt and black pepper. Cook for 12 minutes or until the pasta is tender with a bite and most of the liquid has dried out.
3. Stir in the turkey, spinach, and double cream. Pour the mixture into a baking dish that is good for your air fryer. Mix the cheeses and spread them on top.
4. Set the air fryer to 190°C (380°F) for 15 minutes.
5. Bake the dish in the air fryer for 10 to 15 minutes or until the cheeses melt and are golden brown.
6. Remove the dish, let cool slightly and serve warm.

*Would I call this segment my favourite? It is the definition of super relaxing cooking while allowing you to utilise your ingredients before they go bad. These recipes are a merge of 1-ingredient to 4-ingredient recipes that come together quickly and are probably what you need when sudden hunger pangs strike.*

DON'T FORGET TO GET THE

**TOP RECIPES** FROM THIS BOOK AS

**A FREE DOWNLOADABLE PDF IN COLOUR**

**SCAN THE QR CODE BELOW**

*Just follow the steps below to access it via the QR Code (the picture code at the bottom of this page) or click the link if you are reading this on your Phone / Device.*

1. Unlock your phone & open up the phone's camera
2. Make sure you are using the "back" camera (as if you were taking a photo of someone) and point it towards the QR code at the bottom of the page.
3. Tap your phone's screen exactly where the QR code is.
4. A link / pop up will appear. Simply tap that (and make sure you have internet connection) and the FREE PDF containing all of the colored images should appear.

# APPLE COBBLER

*Servings: 4*

### TOTAL CALORIES: 1117
Protein: 8.46g | Fats: 32.6g | Carbs: 202.27g

## INGREDIENTS

- 4 cups apple pie filling
- 1 stick salted butter, melted
- 1 box white or yellow cake mix

## INSTRUCTIONS

1. Spread the apple pie filling in a baking dish that's a good size for your air fryer. Mix the butter with the cake mix and spread the mixture on top of the apple pie filling.
2. Set the air fryer to 180°C (360°F) for 12 minutes.
3. Place the dish in the air fryer and bake for 10 to 12 minutes or until the top is golden brown and the filling is bubbly.
4. Put the dish on a heat-proof surface, let cool moderately, and serve with ice cream.

# AVOCADO & EGGS

*Servings: 4*

### TOTAL CALORIES: 228
Protein: 7.76g | Fats: 18.94g | Carbs: 9.95g

## INGREDIENTS

- 2 avocados, halved and pitted
- 4 medium eggs
- Salt and black pepper to taste

## INSTRUCTIONS

1. Set the air fryer to 200°C (400°F) for 9 minutes.
2. In each avocado, crack one egg into them and season with salt and black pepper.
3. Carefully put the avocados in the air fryer basket and bake for 9 minutes or until the eggs set to your desire.
4. Remove the avocados onto a plate and serve immediately.

# BLOOMING ONION

*Servings: 4*

**TOTAL CALORIES: 278**
Protein: 10.26g | Fats: 3.9g | Carbs: 49.69g

## INGREDIENTS
- 1 large sweet onion
- 1 cup plain flour
- 2 eggs, beaten
- 1 cup seasoned bread crumbs

## INSTRUCTIONS
1. Cut 1cm (½-inch) off the top of the onion and peel the outer skin. Turn the onion upside down and using a sharp knife, starting from near the root (not too close), cut a slit through from the top to the bottom without touching the middle of the onion. Make four more slits this way. Turn the onion back up to set on its root and gently open up the slit to resemble a flower.
2. Dredge the onion in the flour, dip well in the eggs, and coat generously with the breadcrumbs.
3. Set the air fryer to 150°C (300°F) for 30 minutes.
4. Set the onion in the air fryer with the root side facing downwards and mist with cooking spray. Bake for 25 to 30 minutes or until it is golden brown and crispy.
5. Plate the onion and serve with your favourite dipping sauce.

# BOURBON-BRUSHED PEACHES

*Servings: 4*

**TOTAL CALORIES: 65**
Protein: 1.37g | Fats: 0.38g | Carbs: 14.31g

## INGREDIENTS
- 4 peaches, halved and pitted
- 30ml (1 oz) bourbon

## INSTRUCTIONS
1. Set the air fryer to 190°C (380°F) for 8 minutes.
2. Brush the inner sides of the peaches with bourbon.
3. Mist the air fryer basket with cooking spray and set the peaches in it with the brushed side facing upwards.
4. "Grill" the peaches for 6 to 8 minutes or until they are golden brown.
5. Transfer them to a plate and serve them with ice cream.

## BROWN SUGAR BANANAS

*Servings: 4*

### TOTAL CALORIES: 78
Protein: 0.75g | Fats: 0.22g | Carbs: 19.95g

### INGREDIENTS

- 2 large bananas, semi-ripe
- 2 tbsp brown sugar

### INSTRUCTIONS

1. Peel the bananas and slice them in halves lengthwise.
2. Line the air fryer basket with foil and set the bananas inside with the seed side facing upwards. Sprinkle the brown sugar on top.
3. Set the air fryer to 190°C (380°F) for 5 minutes.
4. Bake the bananas for 4 to 5 minutes or until the sugar melts and the bananas and golden brown.
5. Transfer to a plate and compliment with other desserts.

## CHEESE CRISPS

*Servings: 4*

### TOTAL CALORIES: 227
Protein: 13.46g | Fats: 18.94g | Carbs: 0.74g

### INGREDIENTS

- 8 ultra-thin slices cheddar cheese (or other cheese of choice)

### INSTRUCTIONS

1. Set the air fryer to 175°C (350°F) for 5 minutes.
2. Line the air fryer basket with parchment paper and place the cheese slices in it with 2cm intervals between them.
3. Bake for 5 minutes or until the cheeses melt and develop holes in them.
4. Lift out the parchment paper with the cheeses and let them cool completely before removing them.
5. Enjoy them as snacks or compliment to other foods.

## 7 CHOCOLATE HAZELNUT MUG CAKES

*Servings: 4*

**TOTAL CALORIES: 371**
Protein: 7.02g | Fats: 19.31g | Carbs: 41.4g

### INGREDIENTS

- 300g (1 cup) chocolate hazelnut spread
- 2 large eggs
- 64g (¼ cup) all-purpose flour or gluten-free flour

### INSTRUCTIONS

1. In a bowl, whisk the ¾ of the chocolate hazelnut spread and eggs until smooth. Add the flour and whisk until smooth. Divide the batter into two mugs.
2. Set the air fryer to 180°C (360°F) for 10 minutes.
3. Place the mugs in the air fryer and bake for 8 to 10 minutes or until the cakes set within when tested with a toothpick.
4. Take out the mugs and let them cool nearly completely. Glaze their tops with the remaining chocolate hazelnut spread.

## CONDENSED MILK CAKE 8

*Servings: 4*

**TOTAL CALORIES: 372**
Protein: 13.05g | Fats: 19.58g | Carbs: 35.25g

### INGREDIENTS

- 1 (400g / 14oz) can sweetened condensed milk
- 60g (¼ cup) butter, melted
- 4 eggs, cracked into a bowl
- 160g (1¼ cups) all-purpose flour or gluten-free flour

### INSTRUCTIONS

1. Whisk the condensed milk, butter, and eggs in a bowl until smooth. Add the flour and whisk until smooth batter forms.
2. Pour the batter into a cake pan (with good size for your air fryer).
3. Set the air fryer to 170°C (340°F) for 35 minutes.
4. Place the cake pan in the air fryer and bake for 30 to 35 minutes or until set within when checked with a toothpick.
5. Remove the pan and let the cake cool in it for 10 minutes before transferring it to a wire rack to cool completely.
6. Slice and serve the cake with your favourite toppings.

## CRISPY HASH-BROWNS

*Servings: 4*

**TOTAL CALORIES: 192**
Protein: 3.92g | Fats: 5.25g |
Carbs: 33.27g

### INGREDIENTS

- 2 medium yellow potatoes, peeled
- 22ml (1½ tbsp) olive oil (standard ingredients)
- 4g 1 tsp) onion powder
- 4g (1 tsp) garlic powder
- 2g (½ tsp) sea salt or to taste (standard ingredient)

### INSTRUCTIONS

1. Prepare a bowl of cold water and grate the potatoes into the water. Stir well, let them set for 20 minutes, and then drain the water.
2. Put the potatoes between paper towels and dry them out as much as possible. Pour the potato shreds into a bowl and add the olive oil, onion powder, garlic powder, and salt. Mix everything well.
3. Spread the potatoes into a small baking dish and place the dish in the air fryer.
4. Set the air fryer to 185°C (370°F) for 18 minutes.
5. Bake the potatoes for 15 to 18 minutes or until their tops are golden brown and crispy, and cooked beneath.
6. Take out the pan and serve the hash browns warm.

## GREEN BEANS WITH BACON

*Servings: 4*

**TOTAL CALORIES: 79**
Protein: 2.57g | Fats: 6.35g |
Carbs: 3.65g

### INGREDIENTS

- 2 bundles green beans, trimmed and cut into thirds
- 2 bacon slices, chopped
- 5ml (1 tsp) olive oil (standard ingredient)
- 14g (1 tbsp) chopped fresh parsley for garnish

### INSTRUCTIONS

1. Set the air fryer to 200°C (400°F) for 10 minutes.
2. In a bowl, mix the green beans, bacon, and olive oil.
3. Line the air fryer basket with foil and add the green beans mix.
4. Bake for 10 to 12 minutes or until the bacon is golden brown and the green beans are tender.
5. Spoon the green beans and bacon onto a platter and garnish with parsley. Serve warm.

## GRILLED CAKE

*Servings: 4*

**TOTAL CALORIES: 160**
Protein: 3.06g | Fats: 0.68g | Carbs: 34.59 g

### INGREDIENTS

- 4 (3cm / 1-in) slices pound cake

### INSTRUCTIONS

1. Set the air fryer to 170°C (340°F) for 6 minutes.
2. Mist the air fryer basket with cooking spray, lay the cake slices in it in a single layer, and mist again with cooking spray.
3. "Grill" the cake for 2 to 3 minutes per side or until they are golden brown.
4. Transfer them to a plate and serve them as desserts.

## GRILLED PINEAPPLE

*Servings: 4*

**TOTAL CALORIES: 113**
Protein: 1.22g | Fats: 0.27g | Carbs: 29.68g

### INGREDIENTS

- 1 medium pineapple, peeled and cored

### INSTRUCTIONS

1. Slice the pineapple into 3cm (1-in) rounds.
2. Set the air fryer to 190°C (380°F) for 8 minutes.
3. Mist the air fryer basket with cooking spray, lay the pineapple slices in it without overlapping, and mist again with cooking spray.
4. "Grill" the pineapples for 3 to 4 minutes per side or until they are golden brown.
5. Transfer them to a plate and serve them with desserts.

## GRILLED WATER-MELON

*Servings: 4*

**TOTAL CALORIES: 0**
Protein: 0.01g | Fats: 0g |
Carbs: 0.12g

### INGREDIENTS

- ½ watermelon

### INSTRUCTIONS

1. Cut the watermelon into 4cm (1.5-in) wedges and deseed them as much as possible.
2. Set the air fryer to 190°C (380°F) for 12 minutes.
3. Mist the air fryer basket with cooking spray, lay the watermelon in it in a single layer, and mist again with cooking spray.
4. "Grill" the watermelon for 5 to 6 minutes per side or until they are golden brown.
5. Transfer them to a plate and serve them as snacks or with other desserts.

## HONEY-ROASTED BUTTERNUT SQUASH

*Servings: 4*

**TOTAL CALORIES: 150**
Protein: 2.32g | Fats: 0.23g |
Carbs: 39.49g

### INGREDIENTS

- 900g (2 lb) butternut squash, peeled and cut into bite-size cubes
- Salt to taste (standard ingredient)
- 30 to 45g (2 to 3 tbsp) honey

### INSTRUCTIONS

1. In a bowl, toss the butternut squash with salt and honey until well-coated.
2. Line the air fryer basket with foil and add the butternut squash in a single layer as much as possible.
3. Set the air fryer to 198°C (390°F) for 20 minutes.
4. Roast the butternut squash in the air fryer for 8 to 10 minutes, turn them and roast for 8 to 10 more minutes or until they are golden brown.
5. Remove them onto a plate and serve as a side dish.

## HONEY-ROASTED CARROTS WITH FETA

*Servings: 4*

**TOTAL CALORIES: 194**
Protein: 6.39g | Fats: 9.39g | Carbs: 22.45g

### INGREDIENTS

- 30 to 45ml (2 to 3 tbsp) maple syrup
- 4ml (1 tsp) olive oil (standard ingredient)
- Salt and black pepper to taste (standard ingredients)
- 450g (1 lb) baby carrots, heads trimmed
- Crumbled feta cheese for topping

### INSTRUCTIONS

1. In a bowl, mix the maple syrup, olive oil, salt, and black pepper. Add the carrots and toss well.
2. Set the air fryer to 198°C (390°F) for 15 minutes.
3. Add the carrots to the air fryer basket and roast for 10 to 15 minutes or until the carrots are tender.
4. Remove the carrots onto a plate, top with the feta cheese and serve warm.

## LEMON PEPPER CHICKEN

*Servings: 4*

**TOTAL CALORIES: 328**
Protein: 61.26g | Fats: 7.15g | Carbs: 0.37g

### INGREDIENTS

- 4 chicken breasts, skinless and boneless
- Salt to taste (standard ingredient)
- 5ml (1 tsp) lemon pepper or to taste

### INSTRUCTIONS

1. Set the air fryer to 190°C (380°F) for 12 minutes.
2. Season the chicken on both sides with salt and lemon pepper.
3. Grease the air fryer basket with cooking spray, lay in the chicken in a single layer and mist again with cooking spray.
4. Bake for 10 to 12 minutes or until the chicken is golden brown and reaches an internal temperature of 74°C (165°F).
5. Put the chicken on a plate and let it rest for 5 minutes before serving with pasta or vegetables.

## PAPRIKA CHICKPEAS

*Servings: 4*

**TOTAL CALORIES: 149**
Protein: 7.58g | Fats: 3.02g | Carbs: 24.27g

### INGREDIENTS

- 1 (425g / 15 oz) can chickpeas, drained
- 5g (1 tsp) paprika
- Salt to taste (standard ingredient)

### INSTRUCTIONS

1. Pat the chickpeas dry with paper towels and add them to a bowl. Toss them with paprika and a little salt.
2. Line the air fryer basket with foil and spread the chickpeas in it. Mist them with cooking spray.
3. Set the air fryer to 190°C (380°F) for 15 minutes.
4. Roast the chickpeas for 12 to 15 minutes while shaking the basket 2 to 3 times during cooking until they are golden brown and crispy.
5. Pour them into a bowl, let them cool, and serve.

## PEANUT BUTTER COOKIES

*Servings: 4*

**TOTAL CALORIES: 584**
Protein: 20.03g | Fats: 25.53g | Carbs: 75.74g

### INGREDIENTS

- 85g (1 cup) peanut butter
- 85g (1 cup) white sugar
- 1 egg, cracked into a bowl

### INSTRUCTIONS

1. Set the air fryer to 175°C (350°F) for 5 minutes.
2. Whisk the peanut butter, sugar, and egg in a bowl until smooth thick batter forms.
3. Line the air fryer basket with parchment paper and add 1 tablespoon dollops on the top with 2cm intervals between each. Then, use a fork to press down each dough flat.
4. Bake for 5 minutes or until the cookies set.
5. Put the cookies on a wire rack to cool and bake the remaining dough.

## PIZZA CRUST

*Servings: 4*

**TOTAL CALORIES: 259**
Protein: 8.31g | Fats: 2.6g | Carbs: 49.24g

### INGREDIENTS

- 235ml (1 cup) Greek yoghurt
- 170g (2 cups) self-rising flour

### INSTRUCTIONS

1. In a bowl, mix Greek yoghurt and flour until smooth dough forms.
2. Divide the dough into two and spread each one into a circle.
3. Set the air fryer to 175°C (350°F) for 8 minutes.
4. Place one dough in the air fryer basket and bake for 3 to 4 minutes on each side or the crust is light golden.
5. Remove the dough onto a platter and bake the other dough.
6. Use the crust for baking pizza.

## ROASTED BERRIES

*Servings: 4*

**TOTAL CALORIES: 58**
Protein: 0.74g | Fats: 0.41g | Carbs: 14.05g

### INGREDIENTS

- 440g (2 cups) mixed fresh berries
- 10ml (2 tbsp) maple, honey, or agave syrup

### INSTRUCTIONS

1. In a bowl, toss the berries and syrup until well-coated
2. Line the air fryer basket with foil and spread the berries on top.
3. Set the air fryer to 190°C (380°F) for 5 minutes.
4. Roast the berries in the air fryer for 3 to 5 minutes or until they are light golden brown and tender.
5. Pour them onto a platter and compliment them with other desserts.

## ROASTED PEPPERS AND ONION

*Servings: 4*

**TOTAL CALORIES: 56**
Protein: 0.8g | Fats: 3.53g |
Carbs: 5.65g

### INGREDIENTS

- 1 large each red, green, and yellow bell peppers
- 1 medium white onion
- 15ml (1 tbsp) olive oil (standard ingredient)
- 5g (1 tsp) garlic powder
- 5g (1 tsp) dried thyme
- Salt and black pepper to taste (standard ingredient)

### INSTRUCTIONS

1. Set the air fryer to 180°C (360°F) for 12 minutes.
2. In a bowl, toss the peppers, onion, olive oil, garlic powder, thyme, salt, and black pepper.
3. Line the air fryer basket with foil and add the peppers mixture.
4. Bake for 10 to 12 minutes or until the vegetables are tender.
5. Spoon the vegetables to a platter and serve warm.

## SODA CUPCAKES

*Servings: 4*

**TOTAL CALORIES: 430**
Protein: 5g | Fats: 5.85g |
Carbs: 89.42g

### INGREDIENTS

- 1 box white cake mix
- 1 (355ml / 12 oz) can soda

### INSTRUCTIONS

1. Set the air fryer to 175°C (350°F) for 18 minutes.
2. Line 24 muffin cups with cupcake liners and set them aside.
3. In a bowl, mix the white cake mix and soda until smooth. Spoon the batter into the muffin cups.
4. Place the muffin cups in the air fryer and bake for 15 to 18 minutes or until the cupcakes set within when tested with a toothpick.
5. Take out the cupcakes and let them cool in the cups for 10 minutes. After, remove them with their liners onto a wire rack to cool completely.

## 23 STEAK AND MUSHROOMS

Servings: 4

(IN MINUTES)
PREP
10
COOK
12

**TOTAL CALORIES: 203**
Protein: 24.95g | Fats: 10.28g |
Carbs: 1.43g

## INGREDIENTS

- 450g (1 lb) flank steak, thinly sliced
- 85g (1 cup) sliced white button mushrooms
- ½ medium yellow onion, sliced
- 15ml (1 tbsp) olive oil (standard ingredient)
- Salt and black pepper to taste (standard ingredients)

## INSTRUCTIONS

1. Set the air fryer to 200°C (400°F) for 12 minutes.
2. In a bowl, toss the steak, mushrooms, and onion with olive oil, salt, and black pepper.
3. Line the air fryer basket with foil and add the beef mix.
4. Bake for 10 to 12 minutes or until the beef cooks through and the mushrooms are golden brown.
5. Spoon the beef mix onto a platter and serve warm with rice or other vegetables.

*Fixing up a hefty dinner after a long day out isn't often the best feeling. Finding ways to make a quick and easy dinner time that is healthy, tasty, and filling is the way out. With the air fryer, you can organise dinner in such little time while you unpack for the day. Here are some ideas to check out.*

## DON'T FORGET TO GET THE
## **TOP RECIPES** FROM THIS BOOK
## AS
## **A FREE DOWNLOADABLE PDF IN COLOUR**

**SCAN THE QR CODE BELOW**

*Just follow the steps below to access it via the QR Code (the picture code at the bottom of this page) or click the link if you are reading this on your Phone / Device.*

1. Unlock your phone & open up the phone's camera
2. Make sure you are using the "back" camera (as if you were taking a photo of someone) and point it towards the QR code at the bottom of the page.
3. Tap your phone's screen exactly where the QR code is.
4. A link / pop up will appear. Simply tap that (and make sure you have internet connection) and the FREE PDF containing all of the colored images should appear.

# APPLE BLOOM PIES

*Servings: 4*

(IN MINUTES)
PREP **10**
COOK **25**

## TOTAL CALORIES: 734
Protein: 5.98g | Fats: 36.37g | Carbs: 100.22g

### INGREDIENTS

- 30ml (2 tbsp) butter, melted
- 15g (1 tbsp) brown sugar

For the pie:
- 2 pie crusts, store bought
- 3 apples, peeled, cored, and diced
- 110g (½ cup) white sugar
- 30g (2 tbsp) brown sugar
- 3g (½ tsp) ground nutmeg
- 10g (2 tsp) ground cinnamon

For the topping:
- 30ml (2 tbsp) melted butter

### INSTRUCTIONS

1. Mix the butter and sugar and set it aside.

For the pie:
2. Fit one pie crust in the bottom of a pie pan (that can fit into your air fryer)
3. In a bowl, mix the apples, both sugars, nutmeg, and cinnamon. Spread the mixture on the pie crust and cover with the other pie crust. Pinch the edges to crimp. Then, brush half the melted butter mixture on top.
4. Set the air fryer to 160°C (320°F) for 25 minutes.
5. Place the pie pan in the air fryer and bake for 15 to 25 minutes. Halfway through baking, brush the top with the remaining butter mixture and bake until the crust is golden brown and crispy.
6. Take out the pie and let cool slightly before serving.

# BAKED APPLES WITH RAISINS AND RUM

*Servings: 4*

(IN MINUTES)
PREP **10**
COOK **15**

## TOTAL CALORIES: 540
Protein: 5.09g | Fats: 8g | Carbs: 104.21g

### INGREDIENTS

For the glaze:
- 110g (½ cup) dark brown sugar
- 120ml (½ cup) dark rum
- 5g (1 tsp) ground cinnamon
- 3g (½ tsp) ground nutmeg
- 3g (½ tsp) ground cloves
- 3g (½ tsp) kosher salt

For the apples:
- 6 medium apples, washed
- 30ml (2 tbsp) butter, cut into small pieces
- 75g (1/3 cup) porridge oats
- 110g (½ cup) raisins
- 15ml (1 tbsp) maple syrup
- 3g (½ tsp) ground cinnamon
- Rum raisin ice cream, optional

### INSTRUCTIONS

For the glaze:
1. In a pot, brown sugar, rum, cinnamon, nutmeg, cloves, and salt. Mix well and place over low heat. Cook for 3 to 4 minutes or until the sugar dissolves and the sauce thickens. Turn the heat off and set it aside.

For the apples:
2. Core the apples with a quite wide space enough for the filling.
3. In a bowl, mix the butter, oats, raisins, maple syrup, and cinnamon. Spoon the filling into the apples.
4. Set the apples in a baking dish (good for your air fryer) and drizzle the rum glaze all over them, making sure to coat them well.
5. Set the air fryer to 175°C (350°F) for 15 minutes.
6. Place the dish in the air fryer and bake for 12 to 15 minutes or until the apples are tender.
7. Remove the dish and serve the apples with a luscious drizzle of the rum glaze spoon over them.

# CARROT COFFEE CAKE

*Servings: 4*
*Chill time: 30 mins to 2 hours*

## TOTAL CALORIES: 678
Protein: 13.16g | Fats: 29.97g | Carbs: 91.57g

## INGREDIENTS

For the wet ingredients:
- 120ml (½ cup) buttermilk
- 45ml (3 tbsp) canola oil
- 1 large egg, lightly beaten, room temperature
- 105g (1/3 cup + 2 tbsp) white sugar, divided
- 30g (2 tbsp) dark brown sugar
- 5g (1 tsp) grated orange zest
- 5ml (1 tsp) vanilla extract

For the dry ingredients:
- 225g (1 cup) all-purpose flour / gluten-free flour
- 1g (¼ tsp) baking soda
- 5g (1 tsp) baking powder
- 1g (¼ tsp) salt
- 2 tsp espresso powder

Fold-ins:
- 225g (1 cup) shredded carrots
- 60g (¼ cup) dried cranberries
- 75g (1/3 cup) chopped toasted walnuts
- Soft cream cheese for topping, at room temperature

## INSTRUCTIONS

1. Add the wet ingredients to a bowl and whisk until smooth. Do the same thing for the dry ingredients and combine both mixtures until smooth batter forms. Fold in the carrots, cranberries, and walnuts.
2. Pour the batter in a cake pan (with good size for your air fryer) and level the top evenly.
3. Set the air fryer to 175°C (350°F) for 30 minutes.
4. Put the cake pan in the air fryer and bake for 25 to 30 minutes or until the cake sets when tested with a toothpick.
5. Take out the cake pan and let the cake cool in it for 10 minutes. After, transfer it to a serving platter and spread on the cream cheese.
6. Slice and serve.

# CHOCOLATE CHIP COOKIES

Servings: 4

**TOTAL CALORIES: 978**
Protein: 15.65g | Fats: 41.94g | | Carbs: 133.68g

## INGREDIENTS

- 120ml (½ cup) unsalted butter, melted
- 60g (¼ cup) white sugar
- 110g (½ cup) brown sugar
- 1 egg, cracked into a bowl
- 5g (1 tsp) vanilla extract
- 340g (1½ cups) all-purpose flour / gluten-free flour
- 5g (1 tsp) baking soda
- 1g (¼ tsp) salt
- 225g (1 cup) semi-sweet chocolate chips

## INSTRUCTIONS

1. Mix the butter and both sugars in a bowl and then whisk in the egg and vanilla until smooth. Add the flour, baking soda, and salt and mix until smooth batter forms. Fold in the chocolate chips. Chill the batter in the fridge for 30 minutes.
2. Set the air fryer to 163°C (325°F) for 7 minutes.
3. Line the air fryer basket with parchment paper and scoop 2-tbsp size balls on the paper with 2cm intervals.
4. Bake in the air fryer for 5 to 7 minutes or until they are golden brown and set.
5. Transfer them to a wire rack to cool and serve them after.

# GLAZED CAKE DOUGHNUT HOLES

Servings: 4

**TOTAL CALORIES: 628**
Protein: 8.12g | Fats: 13.53g | Carbs: 119.55g

## INGREDIENTS

- 285g (1 ¼ cups) all-purpose flour / gluten-free flour, plus extra for dusting
- 5g (1 tsp) baking powder
- 1g (¼ tsp) salt
- 30g (2 tbsp) white sugar
- 60g (4 tbsp) cold salted butter, cut into small pieces
- 80ml (1/3 cup) milk
- Cooking spray
- 225g (1 cup) icing sugar
- 45ml (3 tbsp) water

## INSTRUCTIONS

1. In a bowl, mix the flour, baking powder, salt, and sugar. Add the butter and mix with a pastry cutter until finely crumbly. Add the milk and mix until the dough forms into a ball.
2. Dust a working surface and knead the dough on it for about 30 seconds or until the dough is smooth and forms into a cohesive ball. Cut the dough into 14 equal pieces and roll each one into a smooth ball.
3. Set the air fryer to 175°C (350°F) for 10 minutes.
4. Grease the air fryer basket with cooking spray and place the dough balls in it in a single layer. Bake for 8 to 10 minutes or until they are brown and puffed up.
5. Transfer them to a wire rack to cool.
6. In a bowl, mix the powdered sugar and water until smooth to make the glaze.
7. Roll each dough ball in the glaze until well-coated and place on the wire rack to dry.

*THE UK AIR FRYER COOKBOOK*

## JAM ROLY POLY

*Servings: 4*

**TOTAL CALORIES: 421**
Protein: 5.32g | Fats: 12.12g |
Carbs: 72.65g

### INGREDIENTS

- 175g (¾ cup) all-purpose flour / gluten-free flour
- 50g (1/6 cup) caster sugar
- 1g (¼ tsp) salt
- 85g (3 oz) vegetable suet
- 85ml (1/3 cup) cold milk
- 150g (2/3 cup) jam of choice

### INSTRUCTIONS

1. In a bowl, mix the flour, sugar, salt, and suet with a fork. Mix in the cold milk with a fork until the loose paste forms and then mix well with your hands until loose dough forms.
2. Transfer the dough to a floured surface and knead for a few minutes until the dough is smooth. Roll out the dough into a rectangular shape. Use a knife to trim the edges to smooth out the rectangle.
3. Spread the jam on the dough leaving 3cm (1 inch) space of the dough for sealing. Start by rolling the dough over the jam, first tightly and then loosely to the end. Slice the roly poly into 4cm slices. Fit the slices into a baking dish (that can fit into your air fryer).
4. Set the air fryer to 180°C (360°F) for 50 minutes.
5. Put the baking dish in the air fryer and bake for 40 to 50 minutes or until the dough is golden brown and cooked through.
6. Take out the pan and let cool.

## PEACH DUMP CAKE

*Servings: 4*

**TOTAL CALORIES: 430**
Protein: 4.2g | Fats: 25.69g |
Carbs: 50.39g

### INGREDIENTS

- 2 (425g / 15 oz) cans peaches with juice
- 75g (1/3 cup) white cake mix
- 1 stick butter, melted
- Vanilla ice cream for serving

### INSTRUCTIONS

1. Grease a baking dish (with size good enough for your air fryer) with cooking spray. Spread the peaches in the baking dish with a few tbsp of the canning juice. Sprinkle on the cake mix and drizzle the butter on top.
2. Set the air fryer to 163°C (325°F) for 20 minutes.
3. Place the baking dish in the oven and bake for 15 to 20 minutes or until the cake is golden brown and the peach liquid is bubbly.
4. Take out the baking dish and let the cake cool.
5. Serve the cake with ice cream.

## PINEAPPLE UPSIDE DOWN CAKE

*Servings: 4*

(IN MINUTES)
PREP **10**
COOK **25**

**TOTAL CALORIES: 719**
Protein: 7g | Fats: 13.47g | Carbs: 145.41g

### INGREDIENTS

- 1 (500g / 18.05 oz) package cake mix yellow or white
- (also add the ingredients required for the cake mix)
- 30g (2 tbsp) butter, melted
- 570g (20 oz) canned pineapple
- 60g (¼ cup) brown sugar
- 3 maraschino cherries

### INSTRUCTIONS

1. Prepare the cake mix according to the package's instructions.
2. In a round cake pan (good enough for your air fryer), spread the butter and then sprinkle the brown sugar on top. Layer the pineapple on the sugar and decorate with the cherries. Pour the cake batter on top.
3. Set the air fryer to 160°C (320°F) for 25 minutes.
4. Place the cake pan in the air fryer and bake for 25 minutes or until the cake sets when tested with a toothpick.
5. Remove the cake pan and let cool for 10 minutes. Invert the cake onto a serving platter, slice, and serve.

## RHUBARB CRUMBLE

*Servings: 4*

(IN MINUTES)
PREP **15**
COOK **45**

**TOTAL CALORIES: 507**
Protein: 6.68g | Fats: 21.54g | Carbs: 70.39g

### INGREDIENTS

- 400g (2/3 lb) rhubarb
- 100g (½ cup) cold salted butter, cubed
- 150g (½ cup + 2 tbsp) all-purpose flour / gluten-free flour
- 40g (3 tbsp) porridge oats
- 5ml (1 tsp) vanilla extract
- 120g (½ cup + ½ tbsp) caster sugar

### INSTRUCTIONS

1. Wash and trim the ends of the rhubarb and cut into 2cm pieces. Spread the rhubarb into a baking dish (for your air fryer).
2. In a bowl, mix the flour and butter until largely crumbly. Stir in the oats, vanilla, and sugar until well-combined. Sprinkle the crumble mixture on the rhubarb.
3. Set the air fryer to 180°C (360°F) for 45 minutes.
4. Place the dish in the air fryer and bake for 45 mins or until the crumble is golden brown and the rhubarb is bubbly.
5. Take out the dish and serve warm with ice cream.

## STRAWBERRY POP TARTS

*Servings: 4*

**TOTAL CALORIES: 1138**
Protein: 7.57g | Fats: 43.63 | Carbs: 181.84g

## TOFFEE APPLE BREAD

*Servings: 4*

**TOTAL CALORIES: 1037**
Protein: 22.73g | Fats: 46.43g | Carbs: 135.77g

### INGREDIENTS

- 1 (425g / 15 oz) package refrigerated pie crusts (2 crusts)
- 90g (6 tbsp) strawberry preserves or jam
- 450g (2 cups) icing sugar
- 30ml (2 tbsp) melted butter
- 30 to 60ml (2 to 4 tbsp) double cream
- 5ml (1 tsp) vanilla extract
- Sprinkles for topping

### INSTRUCTIONS

1. Using a pizza cutter, cut each pie crust into 4 equal squares. Combine the leftover dough, reroll it and cut out 4 more equal squares to make 12 squares in all.
2. Spoon 1 tbsp of strawberry preserves or jam on the centre of 6 squares and spread out leaving about 1cm (¼-inch) space around the edges of the squares. Dip a finger in water and moisten the edges of the pastry and then cover the squares with the other 6 squares. Press the edges to stick and then, crimp the edges with a fork. Use a knife to make a small slit and the top of each pastry.
3. Set the air fryer to 175°C (350°F) for 11 minutes.
4. Place the pastry in the air fryer and bake for 10 to 11 minutes or until they are golden brown and crispy.
5. When they are ready, take them out onto a wire rack and let them cool completely.
6. Meanwhile, in a bowl, mix the icing sugar, butter, double cream, and vanilla until smooth.
7. Spread the glaze on the tarts and decorate with the sprinkles.
8. Let the glaze harden and then serve.

### INGREDIENTS

- 3 red dessert apples
- ½ lemon, juiced
- 60g (4 tbsp) golden caster sugar
- 400g (1¾ cup) can caramel sauce
- 6 brioche finger rolls, cut into round slices
- 3 eggs, cracked into a bowl
- 240ml (1 cup) double cream
- 480ml (2 cups) milk
- 5ml (1 tsp) vanilla extract
- Vanilla ice cream for serving

### INSTRUCTIONS

1. Core the apples and slice them into thin rings. Toss them with the lemon juice and 2 tablespoons of sugar. Spread two-thirds of the caramel sauce in a baking dish (good enough for your air fryer) and layer the brioche and apples on top. Dot the remaining caramel over the brioche with bits of the apples showing here and there.
2. In a jug, beat the eggs, double cream, milk, vanilla, and 1 tablespoon of sugar. Pour the mixture all over the brioche and apples making sure to cover well. Cover the dish with plastic wrap and refrigerate for 30 mins.
3. Set the air fryer to 170°C (340°F) for 12 minutes.
4. Remove the dish from the fridge, take off the plastic wrap, and sprinkle the remaining sugar on top. Place the dish in the air fryer and bake for 45 to 50 minutes or until golden brown and the custard has set.
5. Take out the dish and serve with vanilla ice cream.

# STRAWBERRY RIPPLE ARCTIC ROLLS

*Servings: 4*
*Freeze time: 4 hours*

## TOTAL CALORIES: 795
Protein: 18.42g | Fats: 11.1g | Carbs: 166.31g

## INGREDIENTS

- 450g (1 lb) strawberries, plus extra to garnish
- 175g (¾ cup) caster sugar, plus extra for dust
- 900ml (4 cups) vanilla ice cream, slightly softened in the fridge
- 3 large eggs
- 125g (2/3 cup) all-purpose flour / gluten-free flour

## INSTRUCTIONS

1. Add strawberries, one-third of caster sugar, and 5 tbsp of water to a pot. Simmer over low heat while stirring for 5 to 8 minutes or until pulpy. Strain through a sieve into a clean pot and discard the seeds. Simmer the liquid again for 5 minutes while stirring until thickened and coats the back of a spoon. Set it aside to cool.
2. Add ice cream to a bowl and ripple through 3 tbsp of strawberry sauce. Spread the ice cream into a large piece of plastic wrap and roll using the sides of the wrap to shape into a large sausage-like shape. Freeze the ice cream until it is solid.
3. Using two small Swiss roll tins, line them with parchment paper and set them aside.
4. Whisk eggs and remaining sugar in a bowl until thick and fluffy. Add flour and gently fold in until smooth. Equally divide the mixture on the Swiss roll tins and spread out evenly.
5. Set the air fryer to 195°C (390°F) for 12mins.
6. Bake each pastry one after another for 10 to 12 minutes or until golden brown and set.
7. Place two large parchment papers (larger than each sponge) on a working surface and dust with the caster sugar.
8. Invert each sponge onto each paper and remove ining paper. Cover with a damp clean napkin and let cool completely.
9. Once the sponges have cooled, spread about 5 tbsp of the strawberry sauce on each. Unwrap ice cream and divide into equal halves. Place each ice cream roll on one short end of each sponge. Holding the base of the parchment paper, roll the sponge over the ice cream. Wrap the roll in plastic wrap and freeze until solid.
10. To serve, let the rolls soften slightly and slice.

# CHOCOLATE SPONGE WITH CHOCOLATE CUSTARD

*Servings: 4*
*Freeze time: 4 hours*

**TOTAL CALORIES: 1129**
Protein: 32.52g | Fats: 23.27g | Carbs: 222.64g

## INGREDIENTS

- 6 large eggs, separated
- 350g (1 and 2/3 cup) light muscovado sugar
- 120ml (½ cup) date syrup
- 225g (1 cup) all-purpose flour / gluten-free flour
- 10g (2 tsp) baking powder
- 110g (½ cup) cocoa powder

For the chocolate custard:
- 75g (5 tbsp) custard powder
- 50g (3 tbsp) cocoa powder
- 75g (5 tbsp) light muscovado sugar
- 1.2 litres (5 cups) skimmed milk

## INSTRUCTIONS

For the chocolate sponge:
1. Beat the egg whites in a stand mixer until stiff peaks form at the end of the whisk. Add half of the sugar and whisk until glossy and thick. In a bowl, whisk the egg yolks and remaining sugar until the mixture is pale. Whisk in the date syrup and then fold in the egg whites.
2. In a bowl, mix the flour, baking powder, and cocoa powder. Sprinkle the mixture on the wet ingredients and gently fold until well-combined.
3. Scrape the mixture into a cake pan and hit it on a flat surface until it is leveled.
4. Set the air fryer to 160°C (320°F) for 40 minutes.
5. Bake the cake for 30 to 40 minutes or until set when tested with a toothpick.

For the chocolate custard:
6. While the cake bakes, mix the custard powder, cocoa powder, and sugar in a saucepan. Slowly stir in the milk until smooth paste forms.
7. Place the pan over medium heat and cook with continuous stirring until thick and bubbly. Turn the heat off.
8. When the cake is ready, take out the cake pan and let the sponge rest in it for 10 minutes.
9. After, transfer the warm sponge to a platter and cut into slabs.
10. Spoon the custard on top of each slab and serve.

# ROSE CHOCOLATE CAKE

*Servings: 4*
*Freeze time: 4 hours*

**TOTAL CALORIES: 1566**
Protein: 34.04g | Fats: 96.77g | Carbs: 145.61g

## INGREDIENTS

For the cake:
- 170g (6 oz) butter, at room temperature
- 170g (2/3 cup) caster sugar
- 3 eggs, at room temperature
- 5ml (1 tsp) milk
- 170g (6 oz) all-purpose flour / gluten-free flour
- 1 tsp baking powder
- 45g (1½ oz) cocoa powder
- 3g (½ tsp) allspice

- 3ml (½ tsp) rose extract
- 3ml (½ tsp) vanilla extract

For the chocolate icing:
- 200g (7 oz) butter
- 200g (7oz) icing sugar
- 45g (1½ oz) cocoa powder
- 15ml (1 tbsp) milk
- 5ml (1 tsp) vanilla extract
- Edible rose petals, to decorate

## INSTRUCTIONS

For the cake:
1. Cream the butter and sugar in a stand mixer. Crack in the eggs and beat until smooth. Add the milk and beat again until smooth.
2. In a bowl, mix the flour, baking powder, cocoa powder, and allspice. Add this mixture to the wet one and whisk until smooth. Add the rose and vanilla extracts and mix in well.
3. Pour the batter into a cake pan (that can fit into your air fryer) and level the top well.
4. Set the air fryer to 160°C (320°F) for 25 minutes.
5. Put the cake pan in the air fryer and bake for 20 to 25 minutes or until set at the centre when tested with a toothpick.
6. Remove the cake pan and let the cake cool in it for 10 minutes. Transfer the cake to a wire rack and let cool completely.

For the chocolate icing:

7. In a bowl, using a hand mixer, whisk the butter, icing sugar, cocoa powder, milk, and vanilla extract.
8. Spread the icing on the cake and decorate with the rose petals.
9. Slice and serve.

# PISTACHIO PUDDING CAKE

*Servings: 4*
*Freeze time: 4 hours*

## TOTAL CALORIES: 2090
Protein: 25.27g | Fats: 146.21g | Carbs: 184.2g

## INGREDIENTS

- 60g (¼ cup) unsalted butter
- 60g (¼ cup) brown sugar

For the wet ingredients:
- 1 egg, cracked into a bowl
- 60ml (¼ cup) whole milk
- 5g (1 tsp) almond extract

For the dry ingredients:
- 110g (½ cup) all-purpose flour / gluten-free flour
- 75g (1/3 cup) coconut flour
- 3g (½ tsp) baking powder
- 3g (½ tsp) baking soda

- 60g (¼ cup) unsweetened coconut flakes
- 1 (105g / 3.4 oz) package pistachio pudding mix

For the glaze:
- 450g (2 cups) icing sugar
- 90ml (4 tbsp) double cream
- 30ml (2 tbsp) unsalted butter
- 3ml (½ tsp) almond extract
- 110g (½ cup) pistachios, chopped, plus extra for garnish
- 60g (¼ cup) slivered almonds, plus extra for garnish

## INSTRUCTIONS

1. In a stand mixer, cream the butter and brown sugar until smooth and set aside.
2. Combine the wet ingredients in a bowl and whisk until smooth. Do the same thing for the dry ingredients and mix both with the brown sugar butter until smooth batter forms.
3. Pour the batter into a cake pan that can fit into your air fryer, smooth the batter out, and cover the pan with foil.
4. Set the air fryer to 175°C (350°F) for 30 minutes.
5. Place the cake pan in the air fryer and bake for 25 minutes. Remove the foil and bake for 5 more minutes or until the cake sets at the centre.
6. Take out the cake pan and let the cake cool in it for 10 minutes, then transfer it to a cake tray to cool completely.
7. While the cake cools, make the glaze. In a bowl, whisk the icing sugar, double cream, butter, and almond extract. Then, fold in the pistachios and almonds.
8. Spread the glaze on the cake and then garnish with some pistachios and almonds.

# LEMON RASPBERRY POUND CAKE

*Servings: 4*
*Freeze time: 4 hours*

**TOTAL CALORIES: 1572**
Protein: 21.76g | Fats: 43.06g | Carbs: 288.28g

## INGREDIENTS

For the cake:
- 340g (1½ cups) granulated sugar
- 1½ sticks unsalted butter, plus more for buttering the pan
- 3 large eggs
- 120ml (½ cup) lemonade
- 340g (1½ cups) all-purpose flour / gluten-free flour, plus more for flouring the pan
- 15g (1 tbsp) lemon zest
- 1g (¼ tsp) kosher salt
- 1 (170g / 6 oz) container fresh raspberries

For the glaze:
- 225g (1 cup) icing sugar, sifted
- 15g (1 tbsp) fresh lemon zest
- ½ lemon, juiced
- A pinch of salt

## INSTRUCTIONS

For the cake:
1. Cream the butter and sugar in a stand mixer. Crack in the eggs and beat until smooth. Add the lemonade and beat until smooth.
2. In a bowl, mix the flour, lemon zest, and salt. Add this mixture to the wet one and whisk until smooth. Fold in the raspberries.
3. Pour the batter into a cake pan (good for your air fryer) and level the top well.
4. Set the air fryer to 160°C (320°F) for 25 minutes.
5. Put the cake pan in the air fryer and bake for 20 to 25 minutes or until set at the centre when tested with a toothpick.
6. Remove the cake pan and let the cake cool in it for 10 minutes. Transfer the cake to a wire rack and let cool completely.

For the glaze:
7. In a bowl, mix the icing sugar, lemon zest, lemon juice, and salt until silky.
8. Drizzle the glaze over the cake and let dry for a few minutes.
9. Slice and serve.

# GRILLED PEACHES WITH BLUEBERRY BASIL CREAM AND LEMON HONEY

*Servings: 4*
*Freeze time: 2 to 3 hours*

## TOTAL CALORIES: 686
Protein: 8.71g | Fats: 32.31g | Carbs:97.22g

## INGREDIENTS

For the blueberry basil cream:
- 340g (12 oz) frozen blueberries
- 480ml (2 cups) double cream, cold
- 415ml (14 oz) sweet condensed milk
- 28g (1 oz) fresh basil leaves
- 110g (½ cup) white sugar
- 1g (¼ tsp) salt
- 10ml (2 tsp) pure vanilla extract

For the grilled peaches:
- 4 yellow peaches, firm
- 30g (2 tbsp) melted butter
- Fresh mint leaves for garnish

For the lemon honey:
- 120ml (½ cup) honey
- ½ lemon, juiced or taste

## INSTRUCTIONS

For the blueberry basil cream:

1. In a blender, add all the ingredients and blend until smooth.
2. Pour the blueberry cream into a baking dish and freeze for 3 hours.

For the grilled peaches:
3. When ready to have the grilled peaches after the cream has frozen, you can begin grilling.
4. Set the air fryer to 175°C (350°F) for 15 minutes.
5. Cut the peaches in halves and remove the pits. Brush their inner parts with the butter.
6. Place them in the air fryer and "grill" them for 10 to 15 minutes or until they are golden brown.

For the lemon honey drizzle:
7. In a bowl, mix the honey and lemon juice until smooth.
8. Plate the grilled peaches, spoon the blueberry basil cream on top, and drizzle with some lemon honey.
9. Garnish with mint leaves and serve.

# CHURROS WITH CHOCOLATE SAUCE

*Servings: 4*
*Freeze time: 30 minutes*

**TOTAL CALORIES: 504**
Protein: 11.56g | Fats: 16.06g | Carbs: 78.7g

## INGREDIENTS

For the churros:
- 240ml (1 cup) water
- 75g (1/3 cup) unsalted butter
- 15g (1 tbsp) granulated sugar
- A pinch of salt
- 225g (1 cup) all-purpose flour / gluten-free flour
- 3 eggs, cracked into a bowl

For the cinnamon sugar coating:
- 110g (½ cup) white sugar
- 5g (1 tsp) ground cinnamon

For the chocolate sauce:
- 100g (3.5 oz) dark or milk chocolate, chopped
- 100ml (2/3 cup) double cream

## INSTRUCTIONS

For the churros:
1. In a pot, add the water, butter, sugar, and salt. Bring to a bowl and stir until the sugar dissolves. Turn the heat off and mix in the flour until smooth batter forms. Allow the dough to cool for about 5 minutes and then mix one egg at a time until smooth. Spoon the batter into a piping bag with a closed star tip.
2. Line a cookie sheet with parchment paper and squeeze 10cm (4-inch) lengths of the batter onto it with 2cm intervals. Freeze the batter for 30 minutes or until they are handleable.
3. Set the air fryer to 188°C (375°F) for 10 minutes.
4. Mist the air fryer with cooking spray and arrange the dough pieces on top with 2cm intervals.
5. Bake for 8 to 10 minutes or until they are golden brown and puffed.
6. Transfer the churros to a platter to slightly cool.

For the cinnamon sugar coating:
7. Mix the sugar and cinnamon in a bowl and sprinkle over the churros.

For the chocolate sauce:
8. You can do this while the churros freeze or bake.
9. Add the chocolate and double cream to a pot and heat over low-medium heat while stirring until chocolate melts and sauce is silky.
10. Pour the sauce into a bowl and let cool for serving.
11. Serve the churros with the chocolate sauce.

# THE PERFECT BIRTHDAY CAKE

*Servings: 4*

**TOTAL CALORIES: 1291**
Protein: 9.8g | Fats: 80.43g | Carbs: 135.01g

## INGREDIENTS

For the cake:
- 175g (6 oz) butter, at room temperature
- 175g (2/3 cup) caster sugar
- 3 eggs, at room temperature
- 5ml (1 tsp) milk
- 175g (6 oz) all-purpose flour / gluten-free flour
- 5g (1 tsp) baking powder
- 3g (½ tsp) salt
- 3ml (½ tsp) vanilla extract

For the vanilla icing:
- 200g (7 oz) butter
- 227g (8 oz) icing sugar
- 15ml (1 tbsp) milk
- 10ml (2 tsp) vanilla extract
- Sprinkles for garnish
- Cake candles to decorate

## INSTRUCTIONS

For the cake:
1. Cream the butter and sugar in a stand mixer. Crack in the eggs and beat until smooth. Add the milk and beat again until smooth.
2. In a bowl, mix the flour, baking powder, and salt. Add this mixture to the wet one and whisk until smooth. Add the vanilla extract and mix in well.
3. Pour the batter into a round cake pan (that can fit into your air fryer) and level the top well.
4. Set the air fryer to 160°C (320°F) for 25 minutes.
5. Put the cake pan in the air fryer and bake for 20 to 25 minutes or until set at the centre when tested with a toothpick.
6. Remove the cake pan and let the cake cool in it for 10 minutes. Transfer the cake to a wire rack and let cool completely.

For the vanilla icing:

7. In a bowl, using a hand mixer, whisk the butter, icing sugar, milk, and vanilla extract.
8. Spread the icing on the cake and decorate with the sprinkles, and candles too.
9. Slice and serve.

## ABOUT THE AUTHOR

**We are Fearne Prentice!**

A group of Chefs & Recipe Writers decided to team up
and work together to create the best UK Cookbooks
on the market!

See, by working together we can alleviate each
other's weaknesses and create the most delicious
recipes for you to enjoy.

Whether it's needing some UK Air Fryer classics to spice
up your parties, or some slow cooker favorites to warm
your winters we can promise we've got you covered.

We'd also LOVE to hear your feedback and see your
pictures when you create our recipes! Please share
them with us and leave a review!

Now, enough talking, it's time to get back to cooking!

*Don't forget to check out these other books by Fearne Prentice!*

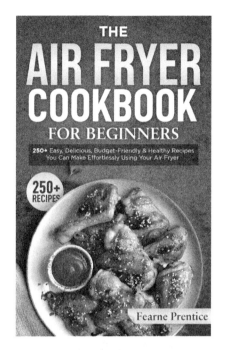

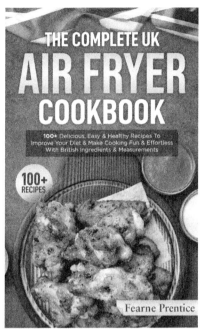

Printed in Great Britain
by Amazon

15823924R00095